'An insightful exploration of systemic inequality, grief and trauma in Black communities. This book offers poignant essays, including powerful narratives on the aftermath of the Grenfell Tower fire, that disproportionately impacted global majority families. It sheds light on the complexities of loss and the resilience of marginalised communities amidst devastating grief and finding ways to heal, juxtaposed with an ongoing fight for Justice.'

– Yvette Williams MBE, Justice 4 Grenfell campaign

'These voices from the Black community emanate compassion, authenticity, outrage and a new vision. We must all heed this drumbeat and review our practice and experience in the light of these truths. Grief is not colour blind.'

– Liz Rothschild, author of *Outside the Box: Everyday Experiences of Death, Bereavement and Life*

'*Black Grief and Healing* is a compelling collection of reflections on the complexities of bereavement and loss in the presence of systemically racist and oppressive systems. Through bringing together a beautiful anthology of poems, stories and essays, the authors provide a deeply moving reminder that there is no one way to tell the story of grief. It is important reading for anyone working to support people affected by bereavement.'

– Dr Sam Royston, research and policy director, Marie Curie

'Blackness and grief have always seemed to go hand in hand, as if by design. Through this timely and important body of work, we can see the shades and textures of grief. This is necessary if we are to know liberation in this lifetime. Incredible explorations and a book everybody should read whether they're Black or not.'

– Kelechi Okafor, author and social commentator

'I genuinely feel this is one of the most important books that will come out this year. The grief as talked about here is overlooked in our society and racism impacts grief a lot. The essays offer many perspectives and talk about many types of grief and how they overlap for the Black community. I recommend white people to read this too but to reflect on this respectfully, bearing in mind that we are here to learn but this is not written for us, and this space is not ours.'

– Jax Davis, Netgalley

T0283170

Black Grief and Healing

Also by this author

Black and Menopausal
Intimate Stories of Navigating the Change
Edited by Yansie Rolston and Yvonne Christie
Foreword by Iya Rev. DeShannon Barnes-Bowens, MS
ISBN 978 1 83997 379 6
eISBN 978 1 83997 380 2

of related interest

Black Again
Losing and Reclaiming My Racial Identity
LaTonya Summers
ISBN 978 1 83997 318 5
eISBN 978 1 83997 319 2
Audio ISBN 978 1 39981 237 5

My Black Motherhood
Mental Health, Stigma, Racism and the System
Sandra Igwe
ISBN 978 1 83997 008 5
eISBN 978 1 83997 009 2
Audio ISBN 978 1 39980 416 5

Therapy in Colour
Intersectional, Anti-Racist and Intercultural
Approaches by Therapists of Colour
Edited by Dr Isha Mckenzie-Mavinga, Kris Black,
Karen Carberry and Eugene Ellis
ISBN 978 1 83997 570 7
eISBN 978 1 83997 571 4

Black Grief and Healing

Why We Need to Talk About Health Inequality, Trauma and Loss

**Edited by Yansie Rolston
and Patrick Vernon OBE**

Foreword by the Rt. Hon. Stuart Lawrence

Jessica Kingsley Publishers
London and Philadelphia

First published in Great Britain in 2024 by Jessica Kingsley Publishers
An imprint of John Murray Press

2

Content Warning: This book covers themes relating to grief, trauma, suicide and loss.

If you're reading this and you have, or have had, thoughts about taking your own life, it's important you
ask someone for help. It's probably difficult for you to see at this time, but you're not alone and
not beyond help. If you need support now, please call your local branch of the Samaritans.

A CIP catalogue record for this title is available from the British Library and the Library of Congress

ISBN 978 1 83997 327 7
eISBN 978 1 83997 328 4

Printed and bound in the United States by Integrated Books International

Jessica Kingsley Publishers' policy is to use papers that are natural, renewable and recyclable
products and made from wood grown in sustainable forests. The logging and manufacturing
processes are expected to conform to the environmental regulations of the country of origin.

Jessica Kingsley Publishers
Carmelite House
50 Victoria Embankment
London EC4Y 0DZ

www.jkp.com

John Murray Press
Part of Hodder & Stoughton Ltd
An Hachette Company

In memory of Yvonne Witter — an activist, strategist, author, colleague, friend, and Ancestor. Her spirit lives on.

Grief, is weighing down heavy

Let's walk with Ancestors

Heed words from learned Elders

Come together as Community

Fight against inequality

Put a stop to generational trauma

Mourn those who have passed

and Heal, we must!

Contents

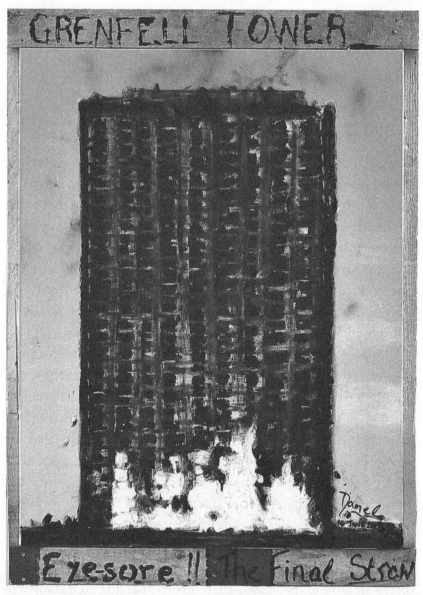

Eye-sore!! The Final Straw © Damel Carayol ST @damel_theartist
www.damel.life

Foreword

Stuart Lawrence

When I think about grief and loss, I often tell the story of meeting Nelson Mandela.

In the first couple of weeks after my 18-year-old brother Stephen was murdered in a racially motivated attack, the news reported that Stephen was a drug dealer, a gang member, someone likely to be murdered because of his affiliations and his way of life. The dominant public voices were trying to lay blame and justify his murder instead of being supportive, to us, the grieving family of an innocent teenager, whose life was brutally taken away.

It was not until meeting Nelson Mandela that the true impact of grief and loss in the face of racism, prejudice and unconscious assumptions hit me. He said that in South Africa Black lives meant nothing, and he realised that in the UK Black lives also meant nothing. It is those few, but very powerful, words that changed our perspectives as a family, and it influenced what was to happen next.

A week later the boys who murdered Stephen were arrested but not charged, and a week after that the government finally began listening to us, his family. The real momentum happened after the change of government – a public inquiry began, and the case became a 'cause célèbre', with news of Stephen's murder being shared all around the world. Then reports that proved instances of racism and bias emerged – some highlighted the way the media initially reported Stephen's death, the attitudes of the police and the general stereotyping of Black people.

Other landmark activities began to happen, but as a family we were not afforded the luxury of having private, quiet time to truly grieve. Instead, we had to focus our energies on fighting for justice for Stephen. Then, in 2011, some justice did prevail when two people were found guilty of Stephen's murder. It was a very challenging time for us, but we were relieved that we had received some justice for Stephen. That justice did not lessen the grief, though; we continued grieving for Stephen. It was hard.

Black grief is not spoken about openly, but I know that when Black people mourn, it is not only for the passing of loved ones. As a community, Black people will also be mourning the systemic inequalities, racial prejudices and oppression that we experience on a day-to-day basis. The truth of the matter is that when a Black person dies in tragic circumstances or because of state injustices, we don't often get empathy from the media, and that complicates the grieving process.

Our family found Stephen's death very challenging; it was very hard on us, but I know that the things that drove my mum and dad on then are the things that drive me on today – to do what I can so that Stephen's death is not in vain. I make it my duty to ensure that losing my brother and all that it has constituted for me will serve some useful purpose.

So, despite my grief, I push on every day doing what I can to try to prevent another family having to experience what we went through. No one else should ever have to go through this level of pain, grief and disbelief while also having to fight for justice. We lived through that as a family because of other people's poor decision-making and the failings of the establishments that are meant to protect us, to be of service to us, and to keep us safe.

We were grieving as a family with the whole world watching us, and my mum and dad tried as much as possible to shield both my sister and myself away from the public eye. It was still very hard because I was seeing things about my family and about a situation I didn't really understand but knew to be fundamentally flawed. That caused a lot of frustration. We were dealing with losing someone we loved and cared for, while at the same time having to face a battleground loaded with heavy armour to fight for justice in a system riddled with racism, bias and prejudice. How were we expected to truly grieve when we were having to prepare for a battle that was unfair, unjust and unwarranted? If only Stephen had not been murdered because of the colour of his skin!

We had to do whatever we could to not get consumed by the grief that was sucking the air out of our body, and instead use that energy to advocate for his, our, your human rights. We were fighting for the basic human right to live and breathe without fear of death simply because of skin colour, and no matter how we were feeling, no matter our pain, Stephen's death could not be vain, so we had to fight on.

But there was, of course, no way that I could lock away that grief forever. Over time I've realised that I went through different elements of grief. I still don't believe I've been through all those elements completely, and I don't think I ever will. After all, I lost someone I love under tragic circumstances. I believe that if Stephen's death was because of natural causes, and he had led a beautiful and full life, then it would have been easier to accept. I also think that there's an easier way of processing that type of grief, but when someone you love is ripped from you for no reason, no reason at all, except because of the colour of his skin – how do you process those emotions? I can't make sense of the loss, and that compounds my grief even more.

I am still trying to cope with the death of my brother, who had so much more life ahead of him, and I don't think I'll ever completely deal with it, or I'll ever completely get over it. It is part of my life, and every day I learn how to live with it. I have good days, I have bad days, and when I have bad days that are tainted with grief, anger and pain, I try to find people around me to help walk me through the emotions and support me. That is why this book is so important.

The authors lay themselves bare, and they bravely, openly and honestly talk about their lived experiences of loss and the social, cultural, political and environmental contexts that impact on grief. I see myself in many of the poems and stories, and as I reflect on the injustices that caused my family and myself so much pain, I realise that we were not even given the common courtesy to grieve properly.

In reading this book it is apparent that even though grief is universal, when it is experienced within a system loaded with generational trauma due to imperialism, colonisation and enslavement, and that is then topped up with the additional layers of structural inequalities and everyday racism, it makes grief so much more difficult to process.

This book is very timely. It cultivates an awareness of the complexities of grief experienced by Black people, and it has given a voice to those who so often struggle in silence. Each poem and story is a compelling read.

Preface

The African diaspora has a long history of being disenfranchised when it comes to health and social care, and we, the editors of this book, are known as activists committed to social justice. We continue to challenge oppressive systems and structures that have been entwined in our own lived experiences of inequality, bias, prejudice, anti-Blackness and racism.

The cold face of the marginalisation and oppression and the shocking levels of disparity endured by the African diaspora in the UK became more evident when the Covid-19 pandemic hit, and we all saw the Black and Brown faces flashing across the TV whenever mention was made of the people who were dying. It was only then that the true impact of the disproportionality and injustices that have silenced Black voices became too obvious to be ignored.

It was so blatant that it raised widespread concern, and the government, communities, academics and individuals began to talk about righting the wrongs. To do that they started to delve into the social and environmental determinants of the inequalities leading to the deaths of Black and Brown people, and that then put the spotlight on the structural, institutional and systemic racist and oppressive systems that intersect with the protected characteristics of gender, disability, age, sexual orientation, religion or belief, marital status and pregnancy and maternity.

But do not be mistaken into believing that the challenges and needs of the Black community in relation to grief begin and end with Covid-19. We were motivated to compile this book not only because we lost loved ones during the Covid-19 pandemic, but because of ongoing systematic social injustices. Historically the Black community has been objectified and dehumanised, and in the UK the state-sanctioned 'hostile environment' policy, the Windrush scandal, increased maternal morbidity rates, the unequal mortality rate for Black men with prostate cancer, long-term sectioning under the 1983 Mental Health Act, the lack of high-quality culturally competent and appropriate therapeutic interventions within mainstream provision and the inadequate funding of third sector organisations providing targeted services are just a few of the ongoing injustices.

When George Floyd was murdered in the USA, the diaspora community was no longer desensitised to the losses of Black lives. That callous murder happened at a time when people in the community were all suffocating under the weight of fear, personal tragedy and trauma, and suddenly there was a collective outpouring of communal grief. The display of grief was not only for the senseless murder of another Black man, but for the myriad of injustices the community have faced and continue to face every single day.

The diaspora community was grieving for the young victims of the New Cross house fire – 13 Black people killed in a racist arson attack while celebrating a birthday,[1] for the 72 victims who were mostly people of colour who died in the Grenfell Tower fire, which, according to Leslie Thomas QC, 'was inextricably linked with race',[2] for those 50 and counting people whose lives were completely ruined by the Windrush scandal,[3] for the deaths in police custody[4] and for so many other injustices. The community grieved for all of them, and found ways to support themselves, each other, and the wider community.

We, together with Helen George, set up BAMEStream,[5] an alliance of mental health practitioners, therapists, policy specialists, organisations, activists and academics, and did a deep dive into mental health and wellbeing services that support the bereavement process for Black and racially minoritised people in the UK. That then led to the alliance offering free, culturally appropriate bereavement support administered by Nafsiyat,[6] which provides therapy and counselling in 20 different languages.

We also set up and manage the Majonzi Fund,[7] providing a monetary grant for people to use towards memorial events and tributes to commemorate the lives of those lost in a way that is meaningful to them, and, with Brian Quavar, set up #UGiveHope, a weekly online platform of entertainment that was triggered by two young Black men struggling with suicidal thoughts reaching out for help. What ensued was a series of 72 light-hearted entertainment sessions of music, poetry, spoken word, magic and comedy performed pro bono by artistes from 31 countries around the world in the spirit of love and unity.

The community does what it can to come together to give hope and to heal.

Notes

1. BBC News (2011) 'Did the New Cross fire create a black British identity?' 18 January. www.bbc.co.uk/news/uk-12182927
2. BBC News (2020) 'Grenfell Tower inquiry: Fire "inextricably linked with race".' 7 July. www.bbc.co.uk/news/uk-53320082
3. Gentleman, A. (2020) '"Lambs to the slaughter": 50 lives ruined by the Windrush scandal.' The Guardian, 19 March. www.theguardian.com/uk-news/2020/mar/19/lambs-to-the-slaughter-50-lives-ruined-by-the-windrush-scandal
4. Afzal, N. (2020) 'Black people dying in custody should surprise no one.' The Guardian, 11 June. www.theguardian.com/uk-news/2020/jun/11/black-deaths-in-police-custody-the-tip-of-an-iceberg-of-racist-treatment
5. www.bamestream.org.uk/bereavement-support
6. www.nafsiyat.org.uk
7. www.majonzi-fund.com

Introduction

Yansie Rolston and Patrick Vernon

When we could not see any anthologies that told the stories of grief and loss through the lens of what it is like to be a Black person in the UK facing a raft of social injustices, we set about curating one.

Grief and bereavement are human conditions, and in many ways, conditions that make us human.

Although grief is universal, and every single person goes through it in varying degrees, the differences in the way in which individuals and communities experience and express grief, and the wide variety of social rules for grieving, are often overlooked. When loss occurs for individuals with pre-existing vulnerabilities it can give rise to acute grief, complicated distress and even depression. Yet, for the African diaspora around the world, and particularly in the UK, despite the social vulnerability, Black grief is often dismissed and not seen on the same footing when compared to other communities or other nationalities.

This is in part because of the history and legacy of enslavement. We were treated and seen as subhuman – sometimes not even as human – and a consequence of this is seen in structural racism, Afrophobia and anti-Blackness, which continues to be experienced even in modern society.

Black Grief and Healing: Why We Need to Talk About Health Inequality, Trauma and Loss is written in a mixture of essay-style personal poignant stories and poetry by people from the African diaspora in the UK whose experiences have been influenced by their multiplicity of social, cultural, political, environmental and, of course, their emotional contexts.

It is purposeful in intention as it takes you, the reader, on a journey into the complex realities of racialised grief and loss based on personal lives; perspectives from academia, movement-building and activism, and from the collective responses that have given hope and created space for healing.

Understanding the historical context of Black grief is important, especially in relation to the stark realities of colonialisation, imperialism, enslavement and ongoing racial prejudices and oppression. Stuart Lawrence's Foreword provides some of that context as he shares his and his family's struggles managing complex grief caused by the racially motivated murder of his brother Stephen. The lack of empathy from the media, having to fight for justice for Stephen and the subsequent public inquiry leading to the publication of the Macpherson report[1] that lay bare deep-seated institutional racism – all had a detrimental impact on the Lawrence family's grief.

However, despite their personal tragedy, the family has provided hope and opportunities for others by setting up the Stephen Lawrence Day Foundation:[2]

> Justice for Stephen is about all of us, every one of us, in society having justice. There are still too many young people who do not have a sense of hope, who just don't get the chance to live their dreams. I want all our children and young people to feel inspired, be confident and have hope in their own future. We are building hope but there is more to do. (Baroness Lawrence, mother of Stephen Lawrence)[3]

Every generation's personal experience is based on the socio-cultural norms of the time, which is displayed in different ways. The stereotypical narrative is that Black people are strong – that they can take it, that they can cope with whatever life throws at them, and when they do grieve, they are often told to 'man up' or 'get on with it' even though grieving is a natural human process. Not being allowed the luxury to grieve in the way that would otherwise seem natural to others, and having to keep one's emotions on hold to get on with the complexities of navigating life as a Black person in the UK does, however, have consequences.

In *Peeping Through the Veil of Grief* Yvonne Christie talks about her own emotionally insulated and insular grief response, and how she eventually became empowered and able to contextualise those emotions after working on the film *Our Grief: Black Women Speak*. Hearing the women's stories gave her the space and opportunity to explore and understand her own grief.

Open Wounds: Vicarious Grieving While Bereaved tells the story of a therapist, Yansie Rolston, coming to terms with the loss of her sister, and how she often suspended her emotions as the grief she was going through became entangled with the grief of others. That interplay of one person's grief with that of another is not unusual, and powerful emotional responses often come out that can lead to inappropriate words, actions or arguments.

It can also add an additional layer of guilt to the grieving stage, which you read about in *Sadness: Losing a Daughter*. Michael Hamilton has a lot of 'if only...' thoughts because of some very unkind words someone said to him. He then speaks of a friend who sat with him, held him, and loved him through the grief. In a turn of events he was a source of comfort for that friend as she battled terminal illness, and he shares the touching story of how he coped during that time.

It goes without saying that multiple losses in quick succession will compound the grieving process, and when that cumulative grief is worsened by tragic events that happen in the community, emotions will bleed from one loss into the other. *A Multitude of Grief* tells the story of such an event where there are losses of family members and friends, and the murder of George Floyd in the USA.

There is Christian, a nephew whose life was celebrated with eating, drinking and dancing through tears and laughter – a cultural norm in many Caribbean communities – and a sister whose funeral was a much more sober event because it happened when the Covid-19 rules said that no more than ten people could attend. Then the moment of George Floyd's brutal murder being shown on TV and on social media on repeat. Thankfully the collective outpouring of support to cope with the community grief helped provide some healing.

We know that culture, superstition and faith are all important parts of personal grief reactions, and *My Jamaican Experiences of Death* gives a glimpse into the customs, rituals and traditions, their meanings, and the roles that they have played in Yvonne Witter's family life in Jamaica. This essay also touches on some of the material conflicts that happen in many families, around who gets what and who takes what when someone passes.

The reality of discord, distress, estrangement and fracture that can occur even before someone passes is also laid bare in Stuart Taylor's *Living in the Liminal Realm: Eulogica* where even though there is love, the entanglement of family disunity is played out.

Grief: Personal Stories from a Black Turkish Cypriot exposes the reader to some of the cultural, religious and social norms from the perspective of a Turkish Cypriot non-practising Muslim, Ertanch Hidayettin, and the comfort he got from receiving culturally relevant bereavement therapy and by attending an ancestral veneration workshop.

Further exploration of socio-cultural intersections is evident in *Death Across Cultures: A Personal Reflection*. The storyteller is a British Nigerian/Jamaican, Chukumeka Maxwell, having traversed from being a child in a civil war in Biafra, Nigeria to living in an area of London known as 'Murder Mile', to being a probationary Christian Buddhist monk, a Quaker prison chaplain, and then founding a suicide prevention organisation – all variables that have influenced his reflections on grief. We know that some of the challenges faced by the community are due to socio-economic disparity, lack of cultural competence, stigmas and taboos, and racial bias and the unfairness of inequalities that presents itself as poor quality healthcare, which invariably impacts on people's life expectancy.

The Black LGBT community in the UK experiences stigma and prejudice on so many levels, and *Black Queer Grief* by Dennis Carney describes dealing with the suicide of a first boyfriend due to homophobia and stigma. Dennis talks about losing many close friends to the HIV/AIDS epidemic, and how not attending funerals and having therapy are all part of his self-care.

Another area of taboo is around young people's grief. *Widowed and Young: Condolences, Rallying and Drying Out* gives context to what it was like as a young Black man suddenly becoming widowed and a single parent to a five-month-old baby and a two-year-old toddler. Tolulope Olajide describes the journey as one initially filled with condolences, the community rallying around with calls, visits and messages, which then dried up after the funeral. When he could not find any services that were specifically tailored for young people, he set up a bereavement charity to help others.

The disproportionality in the racial and ethnic profile of people who succumbed during the Covid-19 pandemic is well documented. Yansie has been involved in carrying out community-based research and Patrick is one of the UK Bereavement Commissioners. Stories of Black people dying unexpectedly during the Covid-19 pandemic were everywhere, and it felt like a tsunami. Many wondered 'Why are we being targeted in this way?', further reinforcing the many conspiracy theories around the causes of the pandemic, and that it was because many people did not, and still don't, trust the system.

Together in Love, Life, and in Death is a personal recollection on what Maureen Anderson considers to be failings in the care system provided to her two parents.

This sentiment is also relayed in *The Rolling Waves of Black Grief* and what Jacqueline Hinds describes as the reluctance of the doctors to refer her dad for exploratory investigations despite his chronic, crippling pain.

The topic is further explored in *Death, Grief, Loss and Bereavement During Covid-19*, which delves into personal and lived experiences and the impact of death on the mental wellbeing of the community during the Covid-19 pandemic. Natalie Darko also provides recommendations on how to better support the Black community.

The disparity is also evident in the statistics on adverse pregnancy outcomes, which is unpacked by Karen Carberry in *Miscarriage, Stillbirth and Infant Loss*. The myriad of inequalities and injustices can sometimes worsen that feeling of a tsunami, especially when there is the double whammy of losing a loved one in tragic circumstances and blatant miscarriages of justice.

Other examples of the gravity of injustices can be found in Sister Isis Amlak's *Suicide in the Shadows of Grenfell* in which a friend, a community activist and campaigner, took her life as a direct result of having to fight against the system, and in Damel Carayol's *The Artist in Grenfell*, about a niece who tragically lost her life in the fire at Grenfell Tower – both grave injustices that have been well documented, both offering some insights into the double whammy of personal grief and community grief, of the state responses, and why, after so many years, there is still no closure.

Black Don't Crack or Does It: The Home Office Scandal is yet another example of the injustices faced by the community. Over the last five years, 26 people from the Windrush Generation have died as a result of the Home Office scandal. Pauline Wilson's death at 64 was as a direct result of that scandal, and because of who she was and what she stood for in the community, news of her passing received national and international coverage, yet the scandal continues.

What we do know, however, is that there is a lot of resilience in the Black community, and NusShen Ankhu's *When Do We Grieve?*

reminds us that we must reclaim the momentum of memory as that will help with healing.

Not All Grief Is the Same: A Funeral Celebrant's Perspective, from Debi Lewinson Roberts, is a clear example of the importance of the role Black funeral celebrants play in paying homage to that memory of loved ones, and the support funeral directors and celebrants provide to those coming to terms with their passing.

In the midst of what feels like a torrent of grief and loss there are many stories of community responses that have helped with the grieving process.

Community Goodwill in Times of Grief: #UGiveHope, from Brian Quavar, relays how artistes from across the Globe came together to help each other to heal during a time of isolation and loneliness.

Reverend Cassius Francis's *Coming Together in Hope: A Service of Reflection* tells of a faith-based response on the National Day of Reflection.

In conclusion, the book tells stories of the disparities of power and privilege and pre-existing schisms and disadvantages, all of which are realities for the community. You will also find some of the powerful ways in which individuals and the community come together to give hope and to heal.

Remember – grieving is human, no matter your racialised identity.

Notes

1. Macpherson, W. (1999) *Report of the Stephen Lawrence Inquiry.* Cm 4262. London: The Stationery Office.
2. https://stephenlawrenceday.org
3. https://stephenlawrenceday.org/stephens-story

Far-Off Farewells

Myrle Roach

Born on the Caribbean Island of Montserrat with a passion for theatre, drama and creative writing, Myrle migrated to the UK in 2002 following volcanic activity on the island. She then began to focus more on creative writing, and has had poems published in an anthology, Brown Eyes, along with articles in regional publications. In 2018 she published her first book of poems, Tamarind Seeds, and has been performing poetry in the Midlands and London under the stage name 'Alliougana Pearl', Alliougana being the Amerindian Arawak name for 'Montserrat'.

Far-Off Farewells

So many farewells were being said
But we were unable to truly bury our dead
They left an unfamiliar world they could no longer call home
To welcoming shores where angels beckon
As we kept our ordered distance from earth's horizon

Unable to say farewell with respect
Give our support in every way correct
Attending wake, nine-night, funeral and reception
We sang our 'How Great Thou Art' from afar
While families stood in isolated solitude around the bier

One by one farewells were being said
As hourly the voracious appetite of the virus was fed
No one was exempt, left out, excluded, rejected or forgotten
A friend, a colleague, an acquaintance, or neighbour
Family member, brother, sister, father, or mother

With 'Amazing Grace' we said goodbye
In the privacy of a personal tearful cry
Unable to hug and view we recalled our last physical contact
We willed the families to feel the love in our sympathetic condolence
As we grieved with them through the distance of our reluctant absence

Such finality in the last farewell
For bereaved living souls it was not well
This unaccustomed isolation is not the life celebration
Accustomed to honour our fallen soldiers and heroes
Now welcomed on high to the realms of heavenly shores.

That Glorious Day

Amanda Inniss

Amanda enjoys creating and sharing her words. Amanda's poem 'A Grip and a Prayer' was selected for the Hackney Council Windrush Generations Festival in June 2020, and her work has been published in Writing Our Legacy Covert *literary magazine. Amanda continues to write and perform spoken word and poetry. Born in Kent to Barbadian parents, Amanda now lives in North London with her three children, and is passionate about older people and community.*

That Glorious Day

> *I know death is not the end*
> *It just really hurts right now*
> *To lose you my dear friend*
> *Your smile occupied such a large space*
> *Now I fill that space*
> *With memories of your face*
>
> *And your words and your jokes and the laughter we shared*
> *I never even imagined for one moment*
> *One day, you would not be here.*
> *You've moved on now*
> *And left us with such a special gift*
> *Being part of the wonderful life, you have lived*

And as I weep and write these very words
I know you are out there,
Looking down on earth
And you will shine brightly
Wherever you reside
Like a twinkling star in the midnight sky

Travelling through time and space
To find your final resting place
I will think of you, as I wipe away my tears
I smile and I know in my heart you will always be near
I'll hold my head up and think fondly of you
Cause I know, you'll be thinking fondly of me too

Rest in perfect heavenly peace
My dear friends
Till that glorious day
When we all meet again.

Leave Me Grief

Amanda Inniss

Leave me grief
and take your numbness too,
I'm finished, I'm done with you.

Why do you persist and come to my door?
Let me be abandoned by you and yours
I no longer need your dreary ways, your feelings of dread
I'm exhausted by the cloud you cast above my head

Leave me grief
and take your anger too,
I'm finished, I'm done with you.

Let my eyes fill one last time
To clear away the storm that rages deep inside Gale force, thunder
    roars
Navigating the hurt, the pain and the months of woe

It may not happen for a while
In my own time my eyes will smile

So leave me grief and take away your blues

I'm finished, I'm done with you.

1 Peeping Through the Veil of Grief

Yvonne Christie

Yvonne describes herself as a woman of substance – mentally and spiritually – who really enjoys a good belly laugh. She is known for having open honest conversations on topics affecting Black women living in the UK and the Caribbean. She has an MA in Applied Psychology (mental health services) and diplomas in counselling and community youth work.

I have recently had the opportunity to work on a film project on the experiences of grief and loss and was able to speak with and listen to testimonies from a group of Black women on their loss.

I've been humbled and excited, yet saddened and empathetic, towards the issues and emotions they have been through, either individually or with their close family members. Some of them are what is colloquially termed 'big women', meaning that they are over 50. They are Black UK-born and raised, work hard, and live rich and productive lives.

Looking back, I notice just how comfortable they all were in wanting to meet and talk about their loss. I marvel at their tenacity, bravery and openness. It felt like they recognised the importance in reflecting on their grief journey and that, for the first time, it also gave many of them the opportunity to record the life and passing of a loved one, even when that passing may have been traumatic or unexpected.

Writing this story will also allow me to lift my own personal veil of truth on my losses and grief because it is all too easy for me to look outwards at other people's experiences without opening up about some of my own anguishes.

Exploring loss often brings up other complex memories. One of the women – early 60s, married for many years, and a mother of three grown children – reflected on being an innocent child playing at her local park with her sister, in the days when youngsters could be on their own in the neighbourhood and it wasn't judged as child abandonment or neglect. She smiles widely at her recollection of the detail of wearing new shoes, and her excitement with the day.

While enjoying her playtime, a white adult male racially abused her and her sister. As she retells the story she speaks of 'still remembering, to this day, the feeling that came over me even now, and that I've never forgotten it deep within my stomach'. She has found the saying 'Sticks and stones may break your bones, but words will never hurt you' to be profoundly untrue.

That awful incident left both her and her sister shocked and dismayed. Aren't adults supposed to care for and look out for children? They were fearful, and trepidation was running through them. How could an adult be so cruel to a child? How could an adult act with so much contempt and dislike towards children who had not done anything wrong? In her mind, adults were supposed to be the people she could rely on to ensure she was safe. Instead, this adult white male had insulted them and, according to her, in that moment she lost her innocence, and the grief she felt for the soiling of her gaiety still sits with her.

As a facilitator of Black voices and experiences it never ceases to surprise me that when you scratch any of our layers, grief is just below the surface. Suppressed, but there, all the same, and it can have an impact on Black people's lives in a negative way forever. This particular woman's children accused her of being paranoid because they didn't understand why she was still so cautious about them travelling the world, but her caution is not without justification. It is based on her own experiences and the invisible hurts, pain and scars. Racism still exists; nothing much has really changed, so she worries about them as Black young people, and wants to protect them from the grief that she has endured over many years.

Another narrator I spent time with left me with a very insightful phrase; she said 'In some cases bereavement begins long before the person leaves this world dependent upon their ailments.' She said that we tend to think there is a linear process that operates when it comes to 'loss, grief and then bereavement', but her experience proved otherwise. Her mother began to live a much-reduced life due to dementia, and so she and her siblings decided that she needed to be moved from her home where she lived alone to live with her, her hubby and her daughters – they had the space and they had each other to draw on for physical and mental support. But her mother's decline over the coming months caused her to grieve, as her mother had slipped away from the person she once was.

Recollecting how the mourning and loss took place long before her mother's body finally left this universe, she said that her daughters took turns to sit with their grandmother, and used the memory they had of their connectedness to stay grounded as their maternal family line slipped further and further away from them all. They all watched her slow demise, and there were many days she didn't even recognise who they were, while at other times she would smile in a far-off, disconnected way.

Her family's bereavement began long before her mother passed on, but having the space and time as a family to be together in a way that wouldn't have been possible if her mother was still living on her own was a very positive thing. It allowed the people who loved and cared for her mother to be there all the time, and that was important because her mother had always made it clear that she didn't want to go into a care home.

As she relayed the story, I could see how quickly and easily she was returning to the emotional place of grief and loss that she occupied. The finale of her recall was her pride in knowing that when her mother finally slipped away 'to the other side', she, and her daughters, were able to fulfil an important Ghanaian cultural ritual of washing and anointing her mother's body with tenderness and love before she left for the chapel of rest. Being able to fulfil those rituals had deep meaning because her mother came from a country where the death and burial ritual was of the utmost importance. The openness and reflections shared helped me to more accurately understand her earlier statement, that bereavement begins for some of us before the loss.

Another of the storytellers has had 11 heart attacks, and there is not a month that passes by where she isn't attending hospital appointments for either tests or updates or to be warded as an inpatient due to pneumonia or some other health crisis such as the chronic arthritis that comes tap-tapping at her door. She is only in her 50s.

She gives up her time, when her health allows, to support and to help others, and makes time to do special Caribbean Christmas food drops with the aid of her family. She says that the food banks do not usually have food that is specific to certain cultures, so she tries to ensure that at least ten families can have a hearty Caribbean dinner. Her generosity is huge, and she feels blessed that despite having had so many heart attacks and complications, she has survived. She says, 'sometimes when I read of other people who have died young, or I get involved in attending another community funeral, I do question why am I still here and these others not?'

This is a prime example of someone who puts aside her own personal grief, and the loss of her previously healthy life, to support others in the large community in which she was born. There was a period of a month when she attended 12 funerals of people she had known closely, including relatives, and she found it incredibly difficult to decide which funeral she could attend. Despite her health challenges, she remains keen for life, but I'm sure that no one would blame her if she stopped for a moment and grieved the loss of her healthy life as she had known it.

As I unveil my own memories of loss and bereavement, I remember my mother who was the matriarch of our bloodline, and who has been dead now for over ten years. Her passing at the age of 86 was unexpected but also not surprising, as over the years I, as many of us do with our elders, watched her dwindling and shrinking. I knew that her epitaph and belief that only God could really take away her breath of life would hold her steadfast, and that when her time came she wouldn't struggle or want to be saved, as bodily and spiritually she was getting weary and tired.

So when her last moments came, and most of us family managed to be by her bedside, I knew that she had done all that she could to pass on what she felt she had to share with us and she could do no more. I was sad but satisfied, and I am convinced that she jumped inside of me not long after her passing. On a daily basis I found myself becoming her, using sayings and phrases that were hers, becoming more honest in my own expressions, which can lead to me being deemed as 'facety' (meaning rude).

But more noticeable to my eyes is that I have become her visually in the mirror. It can happen to the best of us, apparently! My mother is always with me. I miss her. To me she was hilariously funny, and I talk about her often with my daughter who thought her grandma was the best thing since sliced bread, and that feeling was, I believe, reciprocated.

I guess we all have our own level of who we miss the most when it comes to loved ones passing, and the one that shocked and blew me away to a place I didn't recognise was the passing of my sister who at the time was only 48. She was two years and one day older than me, and was the person I turned to for everything. I am not sure she did the same to me, but then, I am younger. Even though it is over 20 years since she passed over, I'm still not sure why and what she died of. She now has two grandsons aged 19 and 16, and who only know of their grandma through their parents' eyes.

They would have loved her. She was fun and very adventurous and bossy and beautiful. She was well loved by her siblings and by the nieces and nephews who knew her before her time came. How did I deal with all the horror and pain that engulfed me and washed over my emotions when the doctor came in to tell us, as a family, that she wasn't going to make it? I am still not sure.

I didn't for one moment expect that she was passing over, and I'm sure that if she was ill now, she would probably be saved – at least I like to think that. They said she had a virus, but it doesn't mean you die from a virus. I don't like to wonder if the hospital gave up on her because she was a Black woman, not knowing what to do or how to treat her, not understanding how precious she was to so many of us. I know for Black people that could be a reality, but I can't even go there, not ever!

That was the first time my mom had to bury one of her nine birth children. She always said it was hard because she had carried her child in her womb, and it was so much more painful for her to bear than when my dad, her husband of 50 years, died that same year.

Peeping through my own veil, how do I explain to people that thinking about my sister can still have me crying? The thought of never ever seeing her in the flesh again can bring me to tears, I mean actual tears, and I'm not a great weeper. Only my sister can take me to the brink in that way.

I still remember some aspects of her funeral, although I was pretty numb at the time. I remember sitting and listening to someone singing, and I just couldn't take it; I thought I was going mad. Have you ever had that feeling, as though your head is going to burst, where you cannot breathe, yet the breath is coming out in loud pants, and everything around you becomes a blur, out of focus, and you want to die right there? These are some of the emotions that I still go through and feel even as I write about these memories, which are still very real to me now.

I guess grief hits us all in different ways. From where I sit and from what I've experienced in life, there are no time limits on when you are supposed to be over it, and even when we have suffered bereavement ourselves, we shouldn't judge how others deal with their loss. I remember talking to someone about my sister who also knew her well, and they scathingly (it felt to me) told me I was 'worshipping the dead'. They said that because I kept talking about her it was like I was worshipping her. Their interpretation of what I thought was a mutual exchange was misconstrued as me worshipping the dead. I know that there are some biblical readings and understandings within various cultural beliefs that make sense to people, but to me it felt insensitive. It came across as though I shouldn't think of her.

This is how some people see things, and even though we didn't fall out over it, it must have hit me deeply somewhere as I still remember the feeling well, yet I can't recall what it was I shared with them about my darling sister for them to respond that way.

Recently I was talking to someone on a deep and meaningful level about my life, and they commented that, 'it is very clear that your sister is a major part of your life, and she is with you always'. That just goes to show that worldviews, opinions and words can either enable people or make them feel guilty, and I believe the latter just shuts people down and prolongs their pain and grief. I have come to understand the importance of being there to listen to people, and to acknowledge that we all carry our hurts deeply and painfully, and, given the chance, it's helpful if they are aired in a supportive way.

I implore us all to hold on to what we believe in. I choose not to compromise my beliefs and be swayed to act in a way that suits others' comfort more than my own. There are individuals and organisations out there that might be better able to understand each of us as well as our cultural norms, so that we can all be heard and understood.

I can honestly say as a Black woman born in the mid-1950s – with the rhetoric of not sharing your business with anyone, which unfortunately also includes feelings and emotions – has meant a deep and long learning curve for me to be able to be open and true to myself. I know different generations have different experiences, but for many of us, those little sayings can still play havoc and we can end up being emotionally isolated and insular. I try to practise letting rip and going for it, and get interesting and funny stares most times. Go on, 'lift that veil right off'.

2 Open Wounds: Vicarious Grieving While Bereaved

Yansie Rolston

Yansie is a health and wellbeing director offering technical expertise to various governments, businesses, civil society and agencies internationally. She is committed and has a cultural sensitivity to the African and Caribbean diaspora and its nuances, and works in Europe, Africa, the USA and the Caribbean designing and setting up culturally appropriate health and social care projects for marginalised people. Yansie blogs, facilitates workshops and seminars, and hosts safe space discussions on mental health and wellbeing; sexual and reproductive health; and the cultural contexts of bereavement, grief and loss. She currently manages the Majonzi Fund,[1] and is Executive Producer of the documentary film Our Grief: Black Women Speak.

What you are reading is a very different chapter to what was intended. It was originally a story about how I had been coping with and healing the wounds of vicarious grief that happened from being constantly exposed to other people's losses. But a sudden turn of events means that this chapter is now about me moving along with grief in real time.

I write this with tears leaking from my eyes, a quiet, whimpering sound resonating in my throat, and a feeling that there is nowhere to hide from this gut-wrenching pain. I do, however, believe that authenticity in the story and my own healing could come from facing the incredible uncomfortableness head on and writing about the emotions as I am experiencing them in the moment. I must admit that I am fearful. I am afraid that this may trigger something inside me that will cause me to sob and sob and sob non-stop until I drop, pounding the floor, worn and exhausted.

She's gone

Something has shifted since my sister passed a few weeks ago, and now the rawness of every interaction takes me to a place I had been shielding from. I had been avoiding the place where despairing sorrow and sadness overstays its welcome, where the days and nights merge into one cloudy overcast blur in the brain, and disconnected robotic movements kick in as the practicalities of life need to be done. I had experienced it before and never wanted to return to that place where the wound of grief is open and raw.

Being a Heyoka empath means that I am someone who feels the emotions and energy of others, and I walk in the shoes of those I support, even when those shoes are clunky and ugly – a bit like Crocs™, really. You see, the ability to intuit with empathy does make it easier for me to help others, but feeling their emotions can be quite draining. To get around this I take time to distil other people's reality from my own, but that in itself can be difficult when there's overlap and their reality is entangled with my own.

I have found that as a therapist, sessions with a reflective supervisor have always been an invaluable commodity, and I consider myself fortunate that mine was straight-talking; he understood cultural nuances and was able to provide nuggets of wisdom in times of need. When the overwhelming feeling of vicarious trauma raised its ugly head, we would work through it together. I relied heavily on him. Then he passed, leaving a significant hole in my support system.

I had known my supervisor for decades, trusted him completely, and didn't have to spend time explaining cultural expressions. It's not that he was someone on whom I would dump my feelings, but he was someone who could help me to lighten my load. He gave me tools to help me rationalise my actions and heal my wounds; he gave me space to just sit in silence and be still. Now here I am, stifling with grief, and wishing he was still alive.

The endless stream of phone calls and text messages from friends, family and even strangers are no longer invitations to socialise or exchanges of pleasantries. They are mostly to tell me how grief-stricken they are by my sister's passing, how they are struggling to cope and questioning whether giving into their grief is the right thing. But their loss is also my loss, and just like that our grief intersects.

She is my sister, and we have a closeness that's impenetrable. No one has ever questioned the bond between us, and now I grieve for her, along with everyone else. Through the cotton wool haziness of my mind, I don't know the answers people are seeking from me when they talk about their grief, but what I do know is that we are all unique, and that they will find out that the right thing for them will be what is right for them. As for me, every visit, call or text message means that the wound of grief rips opens some more.

The triggering

In the mix there are some who, because of guilt at their unkindness towards her, expect me to help them with their emotions, and when they speak, I listen. My sister and I shared secrets, so I know their unpleasantness truly cut her up inside. My emotions then become triggered, yet I remain calm and kind, offering those people who caused my sister pain supportive words or gestures, a hug, even a tight embrace.

After her passing I am standing by myself in quiet contemplation, when from behind I hear a voice – 'I can't believe she's gone' – and the arms of the owner tighten around me. I steel myself as they break down into a tsunami of wailing and sobs. Despite my profound discomfort at the intrusion of my personal space, especially by someone who hurt my sister deeply, my first response is of sensitivity, empathy and compassion, and so I embrace them, stroking their arms.

I stay silent and allow them to be with their emotions as their tears and dribble work their way down my arms. At that moment, their yucky bodily moisture doesn't really matter; I continue to hold them, stroking their arms until the sobbing stops. Then I breathe in a large intake of air and I walk away. I go to a quiet space and reflect on what happened, my own tears falling as I wonder if their expression of grief was genuine, a way of them making peace within themselves, or maybe their way of telling me that they are sorry for the pain they caused my dear sister. I remind myself that it is not for me to judge anyone's actions, and so I let the thoughts turn into clouds in the distance.

It's now a few days after my sister's funeral, and shock, tiredness and loneliness engulf me. I skip dinner, get into the shower and stand still while the warm water cascades down my cold body. Time goes by, and the tears flow and merge with the water running off my face.

I have no idea how long I am in the shower, but when I finally step out, I wrap myself in a white towel, sit on the bed and instinctively pick up the phone, scrolling through photos of my sister; when I do that, it feels like I can see, smell and touch her, and I am comforted. There is a photo of the two of us making faces at each other, and I gaze at it, absorbing every detail – the earrings we are wearing, the mischievous expressions on our faces. Then I smile as I reminisce about some of our more comical escapades – like when we forgot to add baking powder or yeast to the bread mix, and then laughed until we cried as we tried to chew the rock-solid, almost inedible, end product that we contemplated giving to the kids for dinner. My sister and I had the best of times together. As teenagers we wore matching outfits (she in pink, me in yellow) and off we went to see the movie *Grease*. We sang every word of every song out of tune at the top of our voices, and then we did it all again the following week, again, in matching outfits.

Then suddenly a ping brings me back to reality; it's another text from a mutual friend who is overcome with grief. I put on a brave, professional voice, which is what I do when I am not in the mood for too much chit-chat. I listen, offer comforting words, and end the call, vowing to check in on the person later. But what follows is a torrent of tears because I miss my sister, and in that moment I just don't know what I can do to heal. The wound is raw and gaping. I try reading, but to be honest my eyes just scan over the words.

I get up and flick the switch, turning the lights out, and crawl into bed, pulling the duvet over my shivering body. My eyes are shut but I see flickers of light through my closed lids. Is it my imagination or is there really a light penetrating through my lids? I open and shut them again, but the flicker is still there. Then, because grief doesn't happen in a vacuum, I see my dad in my mind's eye while thinking of my sister. I smile momentarily. You see, my dad was a larger-than-life character, full of wit and cutting sarcasm. I have a bank of humorous memories of him that allows me to grieve for him and still be happy and laugh and cry.

I open my eyes again, and the green light of the digital clock says it 10:20 pm; then it dawns on me that 10:20 is the day my dad passed – October 20th – and I relive the moment that he took his last breath – how peaceful he looked, the rise and fall of his chest, that last big exhale and then nothing. How we held his hands, cried and said goodbye as a family. How I battled with conflicting emotions – being grateful that he had died being lovingly cared for at home while at the same time being bereft by his passing. 'How dare you leave your family now?' I ask him, and I answer my own question, telling him that I know his frail body couldn't cope anymore. 'Why do you have to die and leave us?' And then I let him know that I am so grateful he didn't live long enough to suffer, and on and on the contradictions rise in my mind, some I can hear myself expressing verbally, others just mere thoughts.

My dad's passing was anticipated yet untimely, which in itself is a bit of a contradiction. For as long as I can remember – I think I was in my early 20s when he began preparing us for his passing, so for 30 years – I had been expecting it to happen. It was untimely because, except for the very occasional unexplained fainting spells and poorly lungs that had plagued him all his adult life, he had been reasonably fit and well. A few years prior to his passing he suffered a heart attack, but with a cocktail of medication had been able to carry on his life as usual.

My dad prided himself on having clean and tidy surroundings. Our family home had a beautiful garden that he diligently attended to every day. He planted vegetables and flowers, tended the hedge and pruned the trees. When he was not doing that he would sneak out of the house for hours on end to visit his friends or to the market to chat with the vendors and buy fruit for his daily smoothie. He was a raconteur, full of funny anecdotes, and he would tell anyone who would listen jokes about weeing himself and having to resort to wearing adult diapers. It was only when he complained of pain in his bladder that he reluctantly went to the GP to have it checked out. The next day, feeling tired, he took to his bed, and ten days after he passed from bladder cancer.

The shock of this untimeliness was articulated by one of his friends who, on hearing of his passing, said, 'Who knew Ali Rolston could ah dead' and another who heard through the grapevine called in disbelief, 'Since I know your father he been saying he's dying, I just can't believe it's true'. It really did take a lot of convincing for many of his friends to accept his passing.

Am I weird?

I had heard so many stories of people sitting with their loved ones at end of life and had tried to visualise those experiences. I sometimes compare what I heard with my own reality. Did they stand at the side or at the end of the bed, did they sit on a chair, or did they climb into the bed and lay side by side, as I did? Who was the first person they gave comfort to? What did they do immediately after?

I do wonder about my own actions. Would people think it weird that soon after my dad took his last breath I played his favourite music, straightened the bed sheets around him, made sure that his clothes were neat and tidy, put a flower on his chest and gave him a spray of his favourite perfume. I did it because in life he had prided himself on his 'sartorial elegance'. He was a proud Black man and hated to look untidy. But who was I doing those things for? Was it to distract myself or a way of keeping busy, or was it because he would have wanted me to do those things? I had so many thoughts and so many questions, but I know that at that time I did the right thing for me.

There was so much going around in my head as I laid on the bed, thoughts drifting between my dad and my sister. At some point, I must have drifted off to sleep, and I only know that because a sudden burst of light switched on in my brain, my eyes opened and my body jumped alert. Just as soon as that happened the energy surge was extinguished, followed by a sense of relief, disbelief, gratitude, fear, sadness and anger. My thoughts returned to my dad and the inner desire he had for me to follow in his footsteps as a pillar of society. He was a giant of a man, and on his passing a friend said, 'Suddenly a mountain that you see every day is no more', and in that very moment I felt inadequate. Had I failed him? That was grief speaking because I remember my sister's voice continually saying, 'Sweetie, we are all proud of you', and truth be told her opinion matters more to me than my dad's, and so, with the memory of her voice, my smile returned.

My sister is one of my biggest cheerleaders, and after her passing I had a different appreciation of just how much I meant to her. Her faith was everything, and growing up she even considered becoming a nun. I found out that whenever I had to travel abroad because of my fear of flying she would reach out to her fellow 'prayer warriors', asking them to offer blessings and special prayers for me, and when I had a health crisis her priority would be to go to church and ask the priest to say a special prayer for me.

We were front and centre of each other's lives, and the day before her passing I told her, 'Babe, take care of you, I will take care of me, and we will both take care of each other', to which she replied, in a surprisingly steady and strong voice, 'Sweetie, take care of yourself please'. The strength of her voice was very unusual because, as her health failed most days, she could muster no more than a few words in between shallow breaths. This time it was strong and determined, and I am strangely comforted as I reminisce on our last words to each other. Was that our goodbyes? Her way of letting me know that her body had given up the battle for life as we know it, and she was no longer capable of looking after it, and that I owed it to her to look after myself? I hold on to that interpretation because the reality of her physical absence is too painful and awfully sad.

Strange things happen

There is a saying that when white butterflies or white feathers mysteriously appear, they are the souls of departed loved ones, and on the day my dad passed, the garden was awash with white butterflies. Our family once owned a coffee factory, and the smell of freshly roasted coffee wafted in the air as two white butterflies danced around us as we buried his ashes in the cemetery. I was initially scared to ask if anyone else could smell the coffee because I have often been teased for having a very keen sense of smell. It was only when first my brother, then my son and my mum, and then my daughter said that they could all smell coffee that I realised it wasn't merely a case of wishful thinking or my overactive imagination.

Now in the weeks since my sister's passing, I have seen many white butterflies and the odd white feather in unusual places. I even saw one inside the airport, and I felt strangely reassured that my sister was still praying for my safe travels.

Most of my adult life I have journaled, and I get great pleasure browsing the shops in December looking for beautiful diaries; even though there are many journaling apps, I feel something special in turning the pages of a beautiful book and taking my time to neatly write my thoughts, ideas and reflections. It is where I put my fears and my nightmares. I can get lost in the writing and I can sometimes find solutions to stuck problems through decanting them out of my head and onto paper. Now for some strange reason, despite numerous attempts at journaling, my tried and tested coping strategy no longer worked. The words get stuck along the way between brain and pen nib, so I end up closing the diary in frustration and scrolling aimlessly through social media, only to berate myself afterwards for wasting time – time when I could be doing more productive things.

One day, while sitting in solitude, my sister's last words triggered something in me, and I recognise that in giving support to so many others I was neglecting to acknowledge that the 'helper needs help'. I reached out and opened up to my spiritual Godmother, who is a psychotherapist with a special interest in vicarious trauma. I told her of my open wound and together we unpacked and tried to make sense of the feeling of intense loss at the severed physical connectedness between my sister and myself.

At the time I am sure it was a two-way engagement – that I heard all she said and that I had responded – but when I try to recall those sessions, it is all a blur, and then confusion and anxiety hits me. I had made some written notes, but the handwriting is illegible. I do remember coming to a point of realisation that even as a trained therapist I am not one step removed from who I am, that I had experienced a lot of loss in a short space of time – my dad, my therapist supervisor, my best friend, acquaintances and my sister – and that it is important that I acknowledge it for what it was. I am bereaved and I must do what I can to take care of myself.

Finding joy

Even though I still struggle to journal daily, penning this chapter has been therapeutic. Most days I will light a white candle in honour of those I have loved and who have passed, and that gives me the space and time to pause and think, to reflect, and to remember them. The number of calls from others who miss my sister has decreased dramatically, and I am better able to feel and express my grief without the entanglement of the emotions of others. I still do have moments of deep sorrow, but I also laugh and find joy.

My sister and I will forever be connected, just not in the way that we have been accustomed to being. Admittedly it will take some adapting to this new way, but her last words are etched on my mind, and I will keep finding ways to practise self-care and self-compassion.

I do not have all the answers to the questions that float around my mind, but I do know that for me, every day is a new day of surviving what was and accepting what will never be again. I will never stop missing my dad and my sister and grieving for the many others who have passed who I hold dear in my heart.

I accept that my life will never be as it was before their passing, but what I do know is that with the passage of time the wound is becoming less sore, that most days a thin layer of scar tissue creates a protective layer over the open wound, and even though sometimes the tissue is stretched and it tears, causing an opening in the wound, I am healing, and I am finding a way to live life that does not include their physical presence.

Notes

1. www.majonzi-fund.com

3 Sadness: Losing a Daughter

Michael Hamilton

Michael is currently a director of the Ubele Initiative,[1] an African diaspora-led organisation empowering Black and racially minoritised communities to act as catalyst for social and economic change. He has been the director of an NHS young people's health project, a popular radio show host of the Health & Lifestyle show on Choice FM and a part-time lecturer in Youth and Community Work. He has led research projects and management, personal development and leadership programmes in Europe, Africa, South America and the Caribbean. The diversity of his work belies its one simple purpose, which is to create spaces where people and communities can facilitate their own change. As a personal, organisational, business or community coach he brings to each assignment a unique fusion of experience, practice, theory and creativity.

Everyone's grief is filled with a different mix of feelings and emotions. Each person's grief is a collection of experience and current trauma, and the creation of a new future with the deceased in a new place in that future. In my grief for my daughter the unexpected and overwhelming feeling was that of guilt. As a parent, if you do nothing else, it is your responsibility to keep your child alive.

Losing a daughter

Conversation with a friend three days after my daughter died:

> T: How are you doing?
> *Me: I'm doing.*
> T: It's hard.
> *Me: It's hard.*
> T: What's hard?
> *Me: I failed.*
> T: Failed?
> *Me: Yes, failed.*
> T: Failed?
> *Me: My job.*
> T: What job?
> *Me: If nothing else you are supposed to keep your children alive.*
> T: That's hard. You will have to live with that.

The guilt impacted more with my daughter being a teenage child because we had not reached what I have since started to call the 'forgiveness spot' – that time when teenagers are recovering from being teens and parents are recovering from the mistakes that we made in the parenting of our teenagers. My daughter dying as a teenager has meant that I have to find forgiveness of both her and myself from within just me.

I remember attending the funeral of a close family friend whose mother had died. The death took place at a time when the family were storming – everyone was angry with each other. No one was talking. If only she had died six months earlier, before the storm, or six months later, after the storm, the feelings of grief would be a different collection of feelings with different weightings. When my daughter was killed, we were most definitely storming. She was angry with me, I was angry with her. Since she died I have had to learn to allow her to grow up. It was 21 years ago. She is 40 now.

Conversation with a family member on day two:

> She: How's your son?
> *Me: I'm not sure.*
> She: How will you know?
> *Me: Watch, try to talk.*
> She: Look after him.
> *Me: Yes.*
> She: You've messed up one, don't mess this up too.

Oooooooooo! I wanted to scream that my daughter was dead because people broke into her home and tied her up and gagged her, and that the gag killed her. I wanted to scream, 'I didn't kill her!' I wanted to scream that she was not being fair. I wanted to scream, but there was a part of me that accepted this way of seeing.

If only I was not divorced from her mum, if only I had sent her to a different school, if only I had been stricter, if only I had insisted that she stayed in my home, if only I had gone to see her that night rather than going to a concert the night she died, if only I...if only I...

Sadness

Sadness is a hard place, It booms and crashes into your life
An event, A happening, A sight of something that holds you
The flight of someone, To a place far from you
Like, Death, It booms and you scream and cry
You ask, Why o why
Why now, Why me, Why them

Why does the earth continue to spin on its axis
When the world has changed?
Why, Why when I am in such pain

Stop the trees growing
Close the shops
Remove the stars from the sky
How can the grass grow when I hurt so much?

After the booming the pain tries to hide
It hides on your body, It hides in your words
It hides in your appreciation of all of those around
It hides in the taste of your food, It hides in your dreams
It hides in your inability to sleep
It hides and it seeps, It hides and it seeps
Into everything you say, think and do

As it learns to hide, it learns to fester
Like a mouldy cheese just silently festering inside of you

The event was so long ago now
The 'how are yous' have stopped
The anniversaries pass
The world has continued to spin
Smiles have returned
Even to those closest to you

But the sadness holds on tight
Touching all that you touch
Infecting all that you do
And the sadness becomes you.

I found my 19-year-old daughter tied and gagged in her flat. Three men and one woman decided that they would steal what was hers because I suppose they thought it was okay to just take what someone else had worked for. They bound her hands and they covered her mouth with gaffer tape, and five days later...12 July 2001.

Have you ever seen a grown man cry?

No, not just shed a tear into the bottom of a glass of beer on a Saturday
*   night because of his fear of ageing and another sign with the*
*   greying greying greying greying hair. But have you ever seen a*
*   grown man cry? Not from his eye but from deep deep deep inside?*
I was feared, scared
But the decision was made
To find what laid
That smell.
Have you ever seen a grown man cry?
No, not just shed a tear into the bottom of a glass of beer on a Sunday
*   night as he sits alone and remembers the fight(s) from which he*
*   fled to put dirty sheets on this new bed.*
I was feared, scared
As I took the tool
And stood on a stool
To remove the glass
To turn the lock
To open the door.
Have you ever seen a grown man cry?
No, not just shed a tear into the bottom of a glass of beer on a Monday
*   night as he buries his head in solitaire to remove the glare of the*
*   silence in which sits.*
But have you ever seen a grown man cry? Not from his eye but from
*   deep deep deep inside?*
Are you here?

Are you here?

Please answer, are you here?

With blood boiling and heart pounding a

New beat.

Are you here?

Please are you here?

Have you ever seen a grown man cry?

No, not just shed a tear into the bottom of a glass of beer on a Tuesday night sitting alone with friends.

Having to keep going – just don't forget to pretend. They need you smiling – they want your joy. Let them see you recovered. Take pride in your boy.

The stench was so solid

I had to cut my way through.

Let it be the bin; let it be the bin; I said let it be the bin.

The place was ransacked

Everything upside down.

The clock is ticking loud

Bang bang bang

No, that's my heart.

Let it be the bin

Please let it be the bin.

Have you ever seen a grown man cry?

No, not just shed a tear into the bottom of a glass of beer on a Wednesday night as he lists the opportunities that pass him by.

As he remembers that he is not good enough, clean enough, whole enough to stop to enjoy to savour.

But have you ever seen a grown man cry?

Not from his eye

But from deep deep deep inside?

Tied hands

Grey skin

I know that top

I know that shape.
Tied hands
Grey skin
I know that hair
I know a face like that sunken thing.
Have you ever seen a grown man cry?
No, not just shed a tear into the bottom of a glass of beer on a
    Thursday night as he remembers feelings which now sit over there
    as he experiences their taunt – come and get me, come and get me,
    as he reaches, they run.
But have you ever seen a grown man cry?
Not from his eye
But from deep deep deep inside?

It's not the bin
It's not the bin
It's not the bin
It's not the bin.
Fight...there's no one to fight.
Freeze...can't stop and see this no more.
Flight... But where is there to run from this?
Fuck!
Have you ever seen a grown man cry?
No, not just shed a tear into the bottom of a glass of beer on a Friday
    night when the week is over and he has to create his own noise to
    slam out the silence, otherwise he is left with his thoughts and with
    some of the feelings remembering their way as they taunt him.
I fell to the ground
And cried
Not from my eye
But from deep deep deep deep inside?
And I don't now know how to stop.

Being in conversation with a dead person was strange to me. My mum first asked if my daughter Adelle had come to me a few days after she died. Considering this as the ranting of an old woman, I pacified her at the time and left it alone, and then one night I had more than a dream – a dream in which we were in the same space, Adelle and I. I could smell her and hear her and touch her and just have that feeling of being together.

She has come to me in my sleep many times since then. Sometimes I am able to hold those times, to not get out of bed, to remain in sleep mode and prolong our times together. I loved these times. I love these times. A friend said, talk with her. Have conversations with her. Speak out loud and listen for her responses.

I talked with you today

I talked with you today
I was surprised how freely it flowed
To talk with you today.

I just used a word
And then another
And then another
And then they joined
Word on word
Sentence on sentence
Paragraph on paragraph
Thought on thought
Question on question
Feeling on feeling.

And then they joined

And into the mix
I felt your tone.
And into the mix
I called your name.
And into the mix
Came the fear to do what the answers begged.
And into the mix came the strength to feel the fear...you taught.
And in the mix came the gifts you gave.
Those gifts you gave that will always remain
Means that you are always here
Because locked in the mix is you.

Losing a friend

When my daughter died, I called my friend Gerry and said, 'You have to help me.' She asked, 'What can I do?' I said that I didn't know but something in me had chosen her to be the one to help me. So she said okay, and we met. We met weekly for a couple of years and then monthly and then weekly and then whenever I wanted to or needed to meet. I talked and she taught me. I cried and she held me. I screamed and she heard me. I felt like I had a place to touch the pain in safety.

And then, one day, after 12 or so years of meeting, Gerry came to me and said that the doctors had told her that her body was behaving badly and that she was going to die. The following year was spent dying with Gerry, unsure about who we were to each other, unsure about who we were now to each other, but knowing that Gerry and I were friends.

This is a selection of poems from me to her as her body behaved more and more badly, until I had to carry her casket to be burned.

Dance (A letter/poem for Gerry, a dying friend)

You are allowed to dance
Standing or laying down or sitting
You can dance whilst you are awake
Or when you are sleeping
You can dance with your fingers
Or your toes
Or your head
Or if it hurts
Just your nose
You can dance with your eyes
Or just your ears

What ever
You use to dance
Make sure you dance
Make sure you find a time to feel
The rhythms and the energy of the songs around you
Create a space when
You can smile and let go
And just
Flooooooooooowwwwwwwwwwwwwwwwwwwwwwww
And exhale

And just for a moment
Whilst you are there
That is if you can find a moment to spare
Whilst you are there
Hug the thanks that I send for you
Hug the thanks that
All around you send to you

Intoxicate yourself with the love
Of those you have created
And us who you have saved

Thank you, my friend,
I dance because of you
When I thought I could dance no more
God or Karma or the universe or Allah or something or someone sent
  me to you

Your love and your listening ear
Poked the rhythm of my soul and reminded it
To dance again

Find moments please my friend
Through this pain
To dance
And if you ever need a partner with whom to share your dance
If you ever need love and a listening ear
I am always here

Find moments please
My friend
Through this pain
To dance
Love always.

Once Gerry had been diagnosed, once the doctors had said the 'C' word out loud, once they gave a time limit on life, it took over each interaction. It took over spaces where frankly it did not belong. How do we say 'Happy New Year' to someone who is dying?

New Year's Message to a Dying Friend

The doctors said your
Body was behaving bad
AGAIN!
Well...

Wow girl we've passed day 365
And guess what
You're still alive
There it is
I've said it

There it is
I've smiled it

There it is
I've cried it

There it is
I've feared it

And my fears have not come true
So, what now is there to want for you?

Well, we could count down to day 365 number 2
But
I could get hit by a bus
Or an unknown weakness in my brain explodes
And then my counting could never end
Oooooooo fuck
What a muck

O yes
I know what to wish for you

Good tidings and joy

Ooo boy
It can't be as simple as that
Can it?

The fact that Gerry was dying didn't take away from who she was, and who she was to me. It didn't undo the excitement of being around her and learning to be me through her. There are so many things that I can say now, there are so many twists and turns, and thoughts and feelings and fears. But there are always so many things to say right now.

There's So Much Tings to Say

I could say that you are smaller than you were, but that would be
    stating the obvious
I could say that I'm feeling sorrow, that I am going to lose you before I
    am ready, but that would be obvious too.
I could say that life is not fair and that I am fed up with losing those I
    love, but yes, that would be obvious too.

I could say that I had assumed that many years from now we would sit
    on the veranda of the National Theatre and drink tea and ponder
    over life
I could say that I am sorry I won't have you for the moments that
    my son and granddaughters need me at my best, for you to gently
    challenge my weaknesses

I could say that as I travel to you now, I know that I should feel a
sharpness in my heart
I know I should only welch at the prospect of this early parting,
because, my friend, you are going to die before any of us are
prepared, or want or are ready for
But as I travel to you all I do as I have always done is look forward to
my lessons
My lessons for my work, well that is obvious
My lessons as a father, well that is obvious
My lessons as a strength giver, well that is obvious
My lessons as a man, well that is obvious
My lessons as a connected, self-examined, well-centred creative, loving
human being
Well, the lessons you give to help me achieve
A fraction of this is...well,
Well that is obvious too

As you touched my hand the last time we met
As I felt the warmth
Of your now fragile Skin
As I took a small breath
To immerse myself
In being connected to you
I remember that the most important
Teacher, healer, thought provoker
Is the security of friendship
And in the security that you
Have heaped on me
I continue to have the joy
Of the prospect, of sharing a space with you
So perhaps I should
Feel a different balance
Of feelings now

Perhaps I should have a
Different balance of behaviour
Right now, I am sorry
But even now when my awareness informs my consciousness
That it is to you
We travel
They tingle
And giggle
And dance
Then prepare
A clean space
For learning new.

The last time I was with Gerry in life was in a hospice in North London. It was three days before she passed.

Gerry is dying

We sat and we talked but she looked like a woman dying
She told me of the reduction of the lumps
The shrinking of the bad
I tried not to be too sad

But her hair was still there
Her concern (for me) intact
Her ability to insist on me living my best of my life
Was still there

We didn't skirt
The elephant (in the room)
This is what's happening
This is going on

When she stood to walk
Stick in hand
I watched the
Pace of her movement
I saw the loss of her size.

I hope that this sharing of my experiences of grief will allow you, the reader, to borrow some understandings, or to find some normality, or to frame some experiences in another way.

I am a qualified mental health counsellor, I am a qualified youth worker, I am a qualified coach. I have spent the past 40 years working with people. What I have learned is to allow people their own frame. To sit with people while they sense make of their own experiences. That the circle is never round. That the circle is never a circle. These lessons carried true for my own grief. The best help came from those who were prepared to just sit with me, hold me, and love me through it.

Notes

1. www.ubele.org

4 A Multitude of Grief: Willelmina's Story

Willelmina Joseph-Loewenthal

Willelmina Joseph-Loewenthal is an African Caribbean lady of mature years who lives in London. Willelmina has been writing poetry, flash fiction and short stories for several years. More recently (because of several short, creative writing courses) she has been submitting pieces and has had a few successes. In her day job, Willelmina is a mental health peer trainer in an NHS Recovery and Wellbeing College, working with people who sometimes experience severe and complex mental health difficulties. Having lived experience of mental health difficulties herself facilitates this training.

Christian

Christian (Chris) was my nephew, but he was four years my senior. We have strange peer groups in my family! Chris was the son of my eldest sibling, Charles (Charlie), and I was my father's youngest. There were 25 years between Charlie and me. Charlie's three eldest children were all born before me, making me an aunt before I was born. Although we formed a peer group, we were a generation apart.

When we were growing up in the mid-1960s, Chris was a brilliant playmate and an extra 'older brother' – smart, funny, brave and daring – and he treated me just like his little sister, even though technically I was his aunt. When the whole tribe of Joseph kids went out together, it was great to have two 'big brothers' looking out for us.

At the age of 62, Chris collapsed in the street one summer's day in 2018. I soon realised how seriously ill he was when he was transferred to the specialist Royal Brompton Hospital for an operation. Not many days after the operation we were informed that his prospects were not good, and they didn't expect him to survive beyond the next 24 hours. We were advised to come and say goodbye to him. Everyone was devastated.

My brother and sister and I arrived on the ward to be met at the lift by two of Chris's children. They took us to the Family Room where I found my brother and sister-in-law with their other children and many of their grandchildren and great grandchildren. The room was very full and warm, so some of us stayed out in the hallway.

Only two people at a time were allowed to be with Chris. His hospital room was frightening, filled from floor to ceiling with machines, with Chris's little bed in the middle. His nurse monitored him constantly. I sat beside him and let him know how much we loved him and how much havoc we were creating in the Family Room as it was bursting at the seams. That would tickle him. As we were leaving, one of Chris's sons arrived to sit with him. I didn't go to bed that night, and around two in the morning, Chris's younger brother rang – he had died. I lit a candle, poured a libation (a drink poured as an offering), and then went to bed.

It seemed that everyone had a hand in arranging Chris's funeral: designing the order of service and liaising with printers, choosing the hymns and readings and liaising with the priest, selecting readers, contributing to the eulogy, writing the eulogy, hiring a hall, contracting caterers, and arranging the DJ. Someone brought the flowers and decorations for the hall, and my sisters and I spent all night before the funeral sewing madras cloth armbands for the male relatives and chokers for the female relatives.

Family and friends packed the church; there was standing room only. I read the eulogy and spontaneously ended my reading with 'Asé' ('Let it be so', Yoruba (Nigeria)), which produced an unexpected chorus of replies. Asé, or Ashe, is a Yoruba philosophy that defines the power that makes things happen and that produces change.

Some nieces had volunteered to prepare the hall and wait for the caterers and the DJ – who was Chris's friend. By the time we returned from the crematorium the hall was transformed, soon filling up with a dozen people to a table. Family and friends ate and drank, and there were tears and laughter. My husband wrote a tribute song and we all joined in with the chorus. The DJ played some of Chris's favourites – great classic reggae and calypso tracks – and some of us danced. It was a life well celebrated.

Stephanie

2020 was a horrible year for many people. My family's share of the grief began when my eldest sister, Stephanie, died on 5th May.

It wasn't Covid-19 that took her from us, but I still blame it. Who knows how much Covid-19 fear affected her cancer, causing her to die in her sleep. Covid-19 caused unnecessary suffering for her children; they were unable to book a timely funeral, having to wait more than six weeks due to spiralling bookings at the funeral directors. Restrictions limited the number that could attend a church funeral, so they arranged one for the graveside. The funeral took place on a warm, sunny day at the end of June, and the gravestones of the long deceased provided camouflage for the living. I don't know how many people came, but I know that it wasn't ten. Stuff Covid! Using a selfie stick, I FaceTimed the service to my daughter in New York.

The entire service was less than 15 minutes. The priest (who looked impossibly young) conducted graveside prayers, and my eldest niece (physically supported by her daughter and cousin), together with another cousin, spoke and paid tribute. Then it was over. For a while people milled around and spoke in low tones and greeted long-lost relatives and friends while the sons and grandsons filled the grave from the neat pile of earth provided by the digger. Our arms ached with the longing to hug each other; even now my eyes fill with tears at the cruelty of it all. My nephews and great-nephews in their white shirts and dress shoes reminded me of my father Charles, their grandfather and great-grandfather, and my eldest sibling Charlie, their uncle and great-uncle. The little digger brought more earth, and the next contingent of sons and grandsons took over. Finally, the grave was covered in a neat mound, and everyone began to cover it with wreaths and flowers.

My brother and sisters and I had ordered a white wreath that simply read 'Sister', and there were some that read 'Mum' and 'Granny'. There were so many flowers that not one inch of bare earth was left uncovered. The children marked the grave with an engraved brass plate until a headstone could be erected. As the last flowers were being laid people gradually drifted away, and only family and close friends remained to share the heartache.

George Floyd

I suppose my experience of public grieving began on 25th May 2020 with the death of George Floyd in the USA, and the trauma of watching him being murdered. As that nine minutes and forty-six seconds sucked away his life, it drained some of my life force, and now I am not the same person. I know this because just thinking about that awful scene makes tears well up in my eyes. How many other people have experienced this? His death threw me into a melancholy that had nothing to do with my mental health diagnosis – it was the result of seeing something that I should not have seen.

In the end it became unnecessary to watch it again and again on screen because it played over and over in my head. The shock

69

and sorrow of George Floyd's death scene changed our relationship, and he became my brother or my son. I was watching the death of a loved one, and at that point, the grieving became personal, and I was bereaved, just like the countless millions of Black and woke people in the world, but I was doubly bereaved.

I Feel Like the Nail

I feel like the nail that was dropped in the dust during the hammering.
Never looked for. Ignored. Accepted as lost.
Never knowing my power to bite into wood, to hold securely.
Time and weather
Rusting my brightness.
I wore my rejection like a cloak of invisibility.
A device that I have hidden behind all these years.

I wipe off years of accumulated dust
And inspect the blood red rust.
Nothing WD-40 can't fix.
Its oily pungency stings my nostrils,
Reviving me.
My intensity is dazzling; I am sharp,
I am pointed. I am valid.
I drop the cloak.

Social media soothes me, comforts me.
There too are images of others, leaping,
High fiving, hugging, weeping.
They are nails too.
We are ready for the hammering.

Albert

In that same June I attended another funeral, that of a fellow Dominican from my parish – a man I had known for most of my life, and the father of a young friend of mine. It broke my heart to hear the grief in her voice when I spoke to her on the phone. She was angry and confused about how her dad had died; she couldn't understand it. She'd left him in the hospital, sitting up drinking a cup of tea, and then she'd been rung later that day by the hospital to say that her dad was failing fast and that she should return to say goodbye to him. That was the first time that I'd heard such a saga from the relatives of the deceased, but it was not to be the last. As far as I know, no one has been able to work it out.

The funeral was at West London Crematorium, which has almost become my second home, as so many of my relatives and friends are interred there. Albert's coffin was draped in the flag of Dominica. A ritual that has become something of a tradition with many Caribbean people, and without even knowing that this was to be the case, I dressed myself in a Dominican headwrap (made of madras cloth), wore a matching mask and carried my Dominican flag handbag. There was another woman similarly attired. My friend later thanked me, pointing out that her dad would have loved that we made the effort for him. He was a very quiet and humble man. Our parish priest, Father Phillip, conducted the service, which was live-streamed, and my daughter was able to pick it up in New York and Albert's sister did so in Dominica. Father Phillip spoke of Albert fondly, and assured us that heaven was made for people like him, and with just a bare handful of people in the crematorium, Albert was 'laid to rest'.

Anthony

At the end of July, I was shocked to learn of another death, that of my friend Anthony, a volunteer in the local wildlife garden and a fellow member of the Oremi Centre, a specialist mental health resource set up in West London to provide advice and mental health support for adults of African heritage. I have been a member of Oremi for many years because of my own mental health needs.

Anthony had been a cheerful and gentle soul who loved working with plants. He'd had the largest Afro that I'd seen in years, which he must have spent hours looking after. He spoke with a soft Glaswegian accent, but in all the years I knew him, I never really noticed his accent. I often stopped to chat to Anthony, and he would be delighted to greet me while I shopped at our local supermarket. Anthony was often to be found sitting in the sun on a bench outside, watching the world go by with one or other of his friends.

Anthony died in June and there had been none of us – his friends from Oremi – in attendance at his funeral. It hurts my soul that he was sent on his way without our loving company and in the company of strangers.

A Quintain for Anthony

For you
Dear Anthony.
I'll miss the gentle smile
Of your greeting at Sainsbury's.
Farewell.

Irving

My cousin Irving was the middle son of my mother's younger sister.

Although five years younger than me, Irving always exhibited the assurance of someone my senior, even when he was in his teens!

Among his other accomplishments, he was a great sportsman, but cricket was his favourite. He was such a lover of the game that when he wasn't working in his profession as a civil engineer, he spent many a cricket season employed at Lords as a steward. How could this big, bluff, outspoken, inveterate sportsman be taken from us so abruptly? Yet this is exactly what happened. A few days before Christmas 2020 Irving went into hospital with breathing difficulties. He died on Boxing Day due to Covid-19 complications. He was only 56 years old. Larger than life and always full of jokes, it is impossible to believe that he is dead, and I still struggle to believe it now.

At the funeral, Irving's widow and their two children in their 20s looked dazed and shell-shocked, as if living through a nightmare, and indeed this was how we all felt, but there was no waking from this nightmare. I read the eulogy, which was streamed to his two brothers and my daughter in the USA, and to his two sisters in different parts of the UK. I felt disembodied standing there at the lectern, a voice taking part in an impossible performance. To convince myself that he was gone, from time to time, I gazed at his photo on the cover of his order of service, his cheeky, laughing face much too alive to be dead.

Carol

Carol was my brother Charlie's youngest child; she was born in 1966 and was like the baby sister I never had. For the last few years she had been very poorly, and during the 2020 lockdowns she had been shielding and only going out for dialysis.

That year had already taken so much from us, and I thought that we'd come through it, breathing a sigh of relief when the year finally ended. How wrong was I? For many weeks Charlie had been very ill and had been hospitalised; we were all really worried about him. His discharge from hospital almost coincided with Carol's death on 1st February, but he was still so frail he wasn't told straightaway. Relief at his homecoming had been marred by this awful news. Covid-19 had taken its toll once again.

We were back at the same church wearing the same sad, shocked faces. This time the number of people allowed at funerals had increased, but Covid-19 still demanded that the mourners spread themselves around the church, so the echoes bounced off the walls. The occasion seemed surreal, like a bad dream on replay. Charlie and his family had endured so much in recent years; it just didn't seem fair.

Up to this day I carry with me feelings of disbelief. I'm grateful that I kept that drawer full of orders of service. The stark reality of holding someone's order of service is a sobering reminder.

Missing

Fragile bodies letting go,
She's gone, he's gone, they've gone.
Leaving me out in the cold,
Shivering, shocked, shook up.

Grief mugged me in broad daylight,
Threatening my composure,
Tearing away my outer casing,
Eggshell fine,
Babies' bones,
Ashes on the breeze.

No prostrate women wildly weeping.
No hugs of reality,
No stories dim with age, unfolded.

No gales of laughter seeping through open windows,
Sliding under doorways
Causing curious neighbours to wonder...
No large pots stewing,
Contents bubbling contentedly.
No small children dashing
Through forests of legs.
No teenagers leaning casually on walls
Wearing squeaky new sophistication,
Far too cool for school;
Nervous in their still ill-fitting adult bodies.
No clink of bottles passed around,
Spirituous liquors having their day.
No libations poured,
No Roman Catholic prayers intoned;
Litanies tripping off our tongues.
No ancestors invited,
No transition marked.
No comfort in our grief.

Lutfa

On the day we buried Irving, I was hit by news of another loss. It was only recently that I came to the realisation that you only have to have met someone a few times for them to have a massive impact on you. I met Lutfa several times before I realised that she was the mother of my niece (in-law).

Lutfa accompanied her friend to several annual seaside trips organised by the Oremi Centre, and for a few years we interacted without knowing our close family connection. Lutfa was a lovely woman – not just physically but also spiritually; she was a beautiful soul, intelligent, lively and amusing. I soon found out that she was a cat person, just like me, and we hit it off almost straightaway. She was a new old friend!

It was hilarious when we both arrived at the civil marriage of her daughter to my nephew and made that amazing discovery. It was such a blessed day. Lutfa was an incredible woman in many ways, not least of which was being widowed at a young age and raising her children on her own. Every day I regret not having had the chance to spend more time with her. Covid-19 took away that opportunity. I grieve for her like an old friend (maybe in another life we did have a long and deep friendship). I miss her presence. What a remarkable lady!

Oremi Remembrance and Memorial Walk

On 28th July 2021 we gathered at the Oremi Centre to honour members who had died during the pandemic. Although Covid-19 had not been the cause of death for all of them, it had taken away their rites of transition. Covid-19 had also taken away our right to honour their passing. It was a day that began with bright sunshine, but by lunchtime it had begun to cloud over, and rain was threatening. Just after midday we gathered beneath a leafy tree outside the Centre.

One of our members (who is a pastor) led the prayers, and calling each of our members who had died by name, I invited those present to bring them to mind, to recall those occasions of joy that we had shared. I made a libation for each. I invited people to call out the names of their loved ones who had died, and we made libations for them too. It was a very emotional experience, but it helped me to feel that they hadn't been forgotten and that we had marked their passing. Afterwards we did a memorial walk up the Grand Union Canal towpath and returned in the pouring rain. It seemed apt.

Edna 'Queenie' Patterson

Amanda Inniss

She twirled in the sun as if she was young, again
Head held skyward, t'was the music that made her move
The calypso and soca tunes from her youth
When Calypso Rose began to sing,
That tune made Queenie move.
The warmth from the Caribbean came as music,
Although over 5000 miles away,
It radiated an energy, that remained in Queenie
And flowed through her that day.
Queenie resided here in the UK, in the red, white and blue,
Like so many of her Windrush Generation
She was torn between the two.
That day as Queenie danced, a crowd appeared,
And as they looked on, Queenie smiled and they cheered
Oh how she continued to dance without a care.
She brought to life the grey stone pavement,
That lay dormant beneath her feet,
Tapping out the joyous rhythms of the soca and calypso beats.
A cream raffia Stetson sat upon Queenie's head,
Providing a touch of shade, from the sun's mild rays.
The sea, still and calm had long abandoned the beach,
Offering acres of sand in her salty absence,
The men sat nearby oblivious to the newly formed dunes, hypnotised by

dominoes, black and white tiles attacking the table, in fine strategic
style,
Fun and laughter echoed and floated in the air,
As jokes, drinks and rotis they all began to share.
A sunny beautiful day,
Along the promenade where Queenie laughed and
Queenie danced without a care.

5 My Jamaican Experiences of Death

Yvonne Witter

Yvonne is an award-winning speaker, author, and enterprise consultant. She has spent over 20 years guiding people across six continents towards their potential. Her passion is in turning ideas into credible and sustainable businesses, and she has worked with various individuals and teams of people to make this happen. Many businesses and organisations that she has advised in the early stages are thriving businesses a decade or more later. Her work continues to contribute to the development of organisations and people, across the micro-business and social enterprise sectors. Yvonne would describe herself as a conscious practitioner, a solutionist. She is a published author of fiction and non-fiction. She loves travelling for the experience of new cultures, creative arts, writing, food and good conversation.

My father's mother – elderly, plump and fair-skinned with soft, silver hair – had died soon after we arrived in Jamaica from London.

I was about 11 years old, and I remember it vividly because that was my first experience of a funeral. I first met my grandmother in October 1968 in Saint Thomas on the east coast of Jamaica when we arrived on a memorable BOAC flight. It was memorable because the prime minister of Jamaica, the Rt Hon. Hugh Shearer, was also on the flight, and as he left the aircraft via a red carpet on the tarmac, I was allowed to walk on it too, and as a little girl I was full of excitement at following in the footsteps of the prime minister.

My father had arrived in Jamaica six months or so before me so he could finish building the family house and receive the shipment of furniture, carpets and stereograms. The 'Front Room' as we knew it was recreated in Jamaica with the porcelain dogs and plastic fruit bowls. My grandmother then lived with us in the newly built house, and I learned a lot from watching her when I could.

But I knew that my grandmother was not too enamoured with me even though I was just a child. Maybe it was because of my darker complexion or that I was not of her son's sperm and therefore not a blood relative – you see, I was adopted. Her son was my adopted father, and his wife, my aunt, was my birth mother's elder sister. I had been living with them in England since my birth, and so when they decided to sell up and return to Jamaica in the late 1960s, it seemed logical that I, their daughter, would accompany them even though there were some people who were simply not down with the whole adoption situation and the notion I would inherit my father's wealth.

When I first arrived in Jamaica my grandmother was active. She would cut coconut into tiny pieces to feed the chickens, and shell corn for them too, and one day I even saw her kill and clean one of the chickens for our traditional Sunday dinner. She taught me a rhyme – 'Let it be free because it caused the death of poor Mary Lee' – and she laughed. Then she told me that a fart should not be suppressed because it could kill you. She went on to tell me the story of a domestic worker who let out a fart in the presence of her masters and went around the room to each one, curtsied and apologised to all of them: 'Sorry misses, sorry massa'.

I was fascinated by everything I heard and saw from the minute I arrived in Jamaica, and practised patois at every opportunity, which my parents frowned at. But my grandmother's health soon deteriorated, and eventually she became bedridden. My father adored his mother, and culturally in those days it was the child's duty and tradition to care for elderly parents, so he took on his share of responsibility. There was also daily domestic help, and her other granddaughters visited, and because my bedroom had two beds, one of them shared my room.

Death rituals

The first time I became aware of death rituals was when my grandmother passed and I attended my first funeral. In those days as a child your head had to be covered for church – if not a hat, then a lace mantilla – and black, purple or white were the only colours worn to funerals. Conservative dresses and men in suits or white shirts and black pants – definitely no garish colours.

Before that I didn't quite understand the death rituals, but I was inquisitive and would listen to conversations. I noticed tape measures hanging over doors at people's houses and overheard women talking about 'fixing' the widow so that the dead husband would not come back to 'trouble' her. I found out that when a husband dies, the widow will often sleep in red underwear, or tie a red string or tape measure around her waist to ward off the dead man's duppy (ghost), which may want to have sex with her in her sleep. It seems to me that most of the rituals were all about not raising the dead, ensuring that the spirit was resting.

Funerals, like weddings, were a time of big family gatherings. Relatives would come from abroad, and in our family they came from England, Canada and the USA. There would be a full house sometimes, with children too, so I had cousins to play with, I got gifts, and generally there was an atmosphere of unity, but sometimes there were quarrels and conflict too. I was so young I didn't know what the adults quarrelled about, and frankly, I was not interested. I just liked to see the 'foreigners' arrive to stay in our homes and receive nice gifts, usually clothing, shoes or trinkets.

Traditionally in Jamaica some people gather every night for nine nights after a person has passed for the 'wake', lighting a lamp to show that the spirit of the deceased is still in the home; others only celebrate on the ninth night. But no matter how it is done, the Nine Night celebrations are a cornerstone of most Jamaican funerals, and is an example of the blending of Christianity and Traditional African beliefs.

We also had the Nine Night celebration when my grandmother passed, and people came to the house every evening for nine nights after she passed. They stayed well into the night drinking rum, playing dominoes and reflecting on the life and times of my grandmother. Some people just came for the socialising, but the tradition is that if the 'yard' is left empty, it is not a good sign because visitors are an indication of love and support for the deceased and the family. In communities where there is not much entertainment, the Nine Night celebrations provide a place to go. It is something social to do and the chance to enjoy the drumming or guitar playing that might happen. As we were seen as newly arrived from England, the locals attending the nine nights were expecting quite a lot of food, and my father certainly delivered.

It was around this time I had an awareness of duppy, or ghosts as they are also known, because I sensed the presence of the spirit of my grandmother in the house. On Saturdays the house would be empty as my parents would leave early to open their restaurant and supervise the staff. The domestic help would be away for the weekend, and sometimes, while sitting in the front room reading a book or listening to music, it would suddenly seem dark inside, and the smell of disinfectant, mixed powders, lotions and potions would waft over me – that same scent that lingered soon after my grandmother had passed on – and whenever it happened, I would run out of the house into the sunshine and head to my parents' restaurant or to a friend's house.

At the time I was only about 11, but I felt strongly that I was not wanted, and believed that the duppy was a sign to confirm what I was feeling, but I did not tell anyone. I just knew what

I experienced was real. I also felt that rejection when my uncle arrived in Jamaica for the funeral. There is an excitement when relatives land in Jamaica for funerals, and I was no doubt gleefully accompanying him and my cousin as he went to visit people he had grown up with in the community before he had emigrated to England in the 1950s. He then introduced me to someone as 'his brother's wife, sister's child', and even though I called him 'uncle' he would not introduce me as 'niece' – yet his daughter who was born the same year as me was such a close friend when we lived in England – we were like sisters until I left for Jamaica at the age of ten.

Situations like this cause funerals to bring up all sorts of issues for me, often quite unexpectedly. At that age I did not know the significance of how my uncle had 'othered' me. Had I known at the time I might have complained to my father because I never forgot how it made me feel in that moment, and decades later, I still recall him saying it and how excluded I felt.

When I became an adult and returned to Jamaica to arrange or attend funerals, I enjoyed sitting with my family in large groups of people from far and wide. I would ask questions about genealogy or the difference between cooking fish tea and fish soup. I sincerely miss those opportunities to congregate in this way, as these traditions have not been passed down to the younger relatives living in the diaspora.

Now, with this current generation, we hardly know each other, scattered as we are across the diaspora, and having parents who are not necessarily connected and united does not help. The passing of my other grandmother – the one on mother's side – seemed to be the last time that such a big gathering took place in the 1980s.

In 1984 I was on a plane ride to Jamaica to see my dad before he passed because I had got the news of his deterioration. I was racing against time, and it felt like it was the longest flight ever. I spent the entire flight hoping that my dad would not die before I arrived, and luckily I got there in time and was able to visit him in the hospital a few times. One day I went to see him, and he was gone – he was no longer there in the bed, and the patient who was in the bed next to him told me that my dad had shouted out 'He is coming now' and those were his last words.

I threw myself into organising my very first funeral and was reliant on a close friend to take me to the funeral parlour to meet the undertakers, and then off I went to arrange for those digging the grave in the cemetery. Thankfully, even though my family were not religious, I had good relationships with the Anglican parish church because I enjoyed the socialisation of church gatherings. I held a wake for my father and did not mind the nightly visits for nine nights, which was expected because he was a prominent local businessman, so naturally many people came to pay their respects.

In Jamaica activities at a wake will vary according to place, class and religious beliefs, but food and drink, including white rum, are a must at all wakes. I, however, chose not to have any Kumina – which is based on an African-Jamaican religion. Kumina has practices that include secular ceremonies, dance and music that developed from the 'beliefs and traditions brought to the island by enslaved people and indentured labourers, from the Congo region of West Central Africa, during the post-emancipation era.'[1]

For some reason, Kumina freaked me out. When one of my uncles died, my aunt had Kumina, and I felt my body and spirit getting drawn into it, which scared me. Kumina drumming can be very powerful, and at the time I felt that if I got right into the heart of the drumming I'd end up in trance. I suspect I have some connection to these African spiritual traditions, which is why I experienced the drumming so intensely. The colonial legacy that wrongly sees these traditions as nefarious has unfortunately had an impact on me, so instead of embracing the Kumina, I chose fear.

The other funeral I attended in Jamaica was my mother's. When she was gravely ill and I found out that she was close to dying, I went to Jamaica to help care for her, and to tend to the business. It was then that I truly realised that death and grieving can bring out the worst in people, and experiencing first-hand the greed and disrespect left me feeling alone and very isolated in the house that I had grown up in.

One day, not long after my mother passed, I got to the point where I could not take it anymore. Someone had come to the house and was helping themselves to my mother's silverware and kitchen equipment, so I turned around, went back to my bedroom, and pushed furniture up against my door, deciding not to come out of my room until the pillaging was finished. I have since learned that behaviour like that is quite common in Jamaica.

Not long after that I held the wake and the Nine Night celebrations, sorted the house, rented out the business and prepared to return to the UK. Both my adoptive parents were now dead, and I was left with the responsibility of managing their possessions and estate. I did not have Kumina at this dead yard either.

Funerals are generally a great place to meet and get to know family and make new friends, and it can be the ultimate celebration of family and their history. There is something magical about seeing babies in arms and elders, and generations in between, all joined together by blood lines and friendships attending a funeral wake and exchanging the richness of oral tradition as people tell stories and we learn about relatives we did not know. Funeral attendees will talk about past events and experiences that they had with the deceased person, remembering them at every stage of their life. These oral traditions are what give us a real sense of place, purpose and belonging. I always felt empowered, sitting and listening to my uncles and aunts, and I miss my elders a lot.

I listened intently to conversations, and asked questions about my grandfather on my mother's side because he died before I was able to meet him, so for me, these gatherings were educational, affirming who I was, and they could be sobering. I found learning about the childhood experiences of uncles and aunts through story-telling priceless, and it is those funeral rituals that have shaped my beliefs and values and encouraged me to appreciate that people are born, and then they die, and that death is inevitable. My grandfather – the father of my birth-father, lived in Oldham, Lancashire, for most of his life, and when he died, I met cousins from Leeds I never knew existed and a whole other branch of relatives emerged. We all chatted at the funeral, enjoyed drinks and meals together, but did not really stay in touch.

My Jamaican experiences of death have been eye-opening and truly educational. I have learned about customs, rituals and traditions and people's behaviours, and I have been taken into rural areas in Jamaica to learn about country life and my family's ties in certain areas. There is a family burial plot on our ancestral land in Jamaica where quite a few relatives are buried. It is like a mini cemetery, and I am looking forward to going there on my next visit to Jamaica, to perform the ritual of pouring libations to give thanks to my ancestors. I might also organise a cookout in their honour.

What we do in between birth and dying is significant, and my ultimate goal is to leave a legacy. I want my life here to have meant something and to have impacted many people in various positive ways.

Notes

1. https://en.wikipedia.org/wiki/Kumina

6 Living in the Liminal Realm: Eulogica

Stuart Taylor

Stuart is a senior innovation and systemic consultant, producer, programme manager, group work facilitator, qualitative social researcher and writer with 30 years' professional experience. He regularly works at senior organisational levels and designs work programmes leading, commissioning and managing multidisciplinary collaborative professional teams. His depth of experience includes: innovation, leadership, diversity, equality, inclusion and organisational development in the corporate sector, the performing and media arts, cultural, environmental campaigning, civil rights activism, mental and physical health innovation, community development, community and higher education and social enterprise sectors. His inspirations include environmental and social justice, service innovation and systems thinking/systemic constellations.

Shock and surprise, even though we knew this was coming. How far is it possible for any of us to prepare for this profound parting? Saying farewell to your mum, your dad, a brother, a sister, your partner or a loved one is difficult. Death is so final. Even when you know it means an end to suffering for them, even though it might have been months or even years in the coming. For some of us the leaving begins a long time before the actual physical parting. Dementia in its various forms is a silent thief of identity and personality, with our presence in the lives of those who are ailing beginning to diminish months or even years before the final stage of their departure.

This becomes even more pronounced as we are charged with their emotional and physical care, alongside managing the complicated business of their lives. Discord, distress, estrangement and fracture can occur so easily and sadly, so commonly, between family members who remain. The obverse of this is also true. For some of us the tensions generated by the slowly or rapidly receding power of those who gave us life acts as a catalyst in reconnecting and reaffirming the ties that bind us as kin. But not always. It's also not necessarily fixed either. Everything that arises as we become drawn deeper and deeper into the kaleidoscopic, emotional maelstrom of elder care as our parents approach the time of their death is exhausting, exhilarating, bemusing, humbling, enraging and some days simply boring and mundane. Has love ever been otherwise?

Abide with Me, a Catholic hymn by Henry Francis Lyte, 1847

Abide with me, fast falls the eventide
The darkness deepens Lord, with me abide
When other helpers fail and comforts flee
Help of the helpless, oh, abide with me.

Shall We Gather at the River, a Baptist song by Robert Lowry, 1864

Shall we gather at the river,
Where bright angel feet have trod;
With its crystal tide forever
Flowing by the throne of God?

Through the substantial part of her career, M had been responsible for safely seeing many, many new lives into the world, ensuring their care and that of their mothers as an NHS midwife. A woman so intimately acquainted with the arrival of new souls. For some, of course, this moment was one of tragedy and loss.

Within this cloud of bemusement, confusion, hurt and anger there has been the solace and succour of contact, renewal and support from so many others in the community. That this level of affection and fondness was not necessarily present among near family has been hurtful. It has also been liberating, knowing that lines of attachment, allyship and entanglement have been so clearly wrought. Where there was ambiguity before, now there is clarity. Where politeness stopped, necessity prevailed in terms of which relationships served and which did not. Who had been present to support and carry the burden of care over so many months?

It's in the intimacies of caring that we recognise the vulnerability of those who have previously been so dominant in our lives. Their own physical needs so prominent. Their weaknesses laid bare. There is a shock to this and a seemingly unending depth to the emotional pull of this tapering away from independence and autonomy towards dependency and frailness. Our own stored-away need for approval, recognition, affection and reassurance become secondary to the compelling and immediate needs of those for whom we now care for. Maybe this is the moment of passing on, the moment of appreciation and understanding of the physicality of love and loving. Not just warm and fuzzy feelings. Actually a gritty, physical, intimate and weighted reality. Dependency. Stubbornness. Compassion. Memory and reflection. Regret, release and forgiveness. All come to play their part as the transfer, the exchange of being cared for to caring for, takes place. A transition that is in equal parts abrupt and slow. Seen and unseen. Acknowledged and ignored. Welcomed and rejected. These 'easy binaries' really have little place in this dance unto death.

From the Caribbean to Wolverhampton. From the fragrant, bright and sun-kissed vistas of the tropics to the cold, claggy and harsh climes of the West Midlands in the UK. What kind of trade was that?

M, 1938–2020. The measure of a life lived over 82 years. Daughter. Sister. Wife. Mother. Grandmother. Great-grandmother. Bus conductor. Midwife. Active Methodist congregation member. Community member. Survivor of racism.

D, 1932–2020. The measure of a life lived over 88 years. Son. Brother. Husband. Father. Grandfather. Great-grandfather. Soldier. Factory worker. Football club steward. Active Methodist congregation member. Community member. Survivor of racism.

Teenage lovers. A life lived fully together. Lives laid to rest together. A completeness.

Some of the observable expressions and dimensions of two lives lived with courage, energy, generosity, humility, love, industry, purpose, pride and service. How to express this inexpressible sense of loss? Such a strange and unanticipated gathering of so few people to say a final farewell to these loved family members. Ten people together in a chapel of remembrance. This brutal fate experienced because of Covid-19. The strangeness of video-conferencing platforms as a means to participate. Then there was the succour of the spontaneous and heartfelt outpouring of cards and letters from the wider congregation and community of Wolverhampton. A balm to family members, to grieving children, grandchildren and great-grandchildren.

'I love you even more. I love you even more. I love you even more.' How deeply moving and impactful to hear these words from a man unused to showing emotion. A reflective space of calm amidst the profound searing pain of loss. Amidst the stress and trauma of conflict among siblings and wider family members. A metaphorical 'death' to several relationships across the wider family system. A rite of passage. Knowing now the weight of adulthood anticipating the standing of elderhood.

One of my then neighbours happened to be a practising psychotherapist and a published writer. Through one of our brief conversations-in-passing, I referred to the fact that mum had died earlier in the month. They invited me out for a walk to talk about my experience of mum's passing, dealing with my family members and managing my own grief. It was an unexpected and welcome act of friendship and neighbourliness.

On reflection, I can barely remember the details of our conversation. The key thing I do remember was my neighbour's suggestion that I keep a journal over the following month. They referred to the practice as 'Morning Pages'. Something in the suggestion resonated for me. Literally, the very next day, and for the following 30 days without fail, the first activity I did on waking was to position myself on our balcony and write 4–5 sides of A4 pages by hand in my journal. I never had a plan or a particular thematic direction in mind. This was a Zen-like process of being spontaneous, present in the moment, as I attuned to whatever aspects of my relationship to my mum, my dad, my siblings, my partner or my children came to my awareness. I simply wrote it down without hesitation, without trying to make it 'literary', without editing, without considered intention. The process of having this 30- to 45-minute period of quiet, introspective, reflective outpouring of memories, insights and emotions was truly liberating and calming. It was a kind of restorative or healing experience. I have to thank my neighbour, for their compassion, insightfulness and wisdom.

What follows are discrete excerpts from that journaling process. What became my 'Mo(u)rning Pages'. The only edits I have made are to protect the identities of people still living and in relationship to me.

06.08.20. Learning that mum had been hospitalised on two occasions in June was not initially so alarming. One thing that wasn't so obvious to me during that visit was the undoubted emotional stress L & B were under, in their part of the ongoing management of the failing health and irreversible decline of B's parents. Our whole family has been deeply affected across three generations.

07.08.20. It's still a massive shock to lose mum. I'm definitely saddened by this dynamic of multiple fragmentation across the family. Dad's business would not have been a success but for her stalwart support and contribution.

08.08.20. It's been over a month now since mum died. The woman who had for almost 57 years been in my life was gone. I promised dad that I would call him the next morning on Friday 26th to check in with him and see what needed to happen next and, of course, to see how he was doing.

09.08.20. I had never heard such anguish in his voice. Dad had seen L & B on Friday when H had arrived; we talked about L & B returning to the family home later that day.

10.08.20. They've learned the rhythms and cycles of dying and all the business that necessarily surrounds death. These included shots of mum's large family of seven siblings and of dad's brothers and his mother and father too.

11.08.20. There was something very tender and sweet – intimate and light too – in the free-flowing exchange of conversation that arose between us all – dad, L, B, H and I – as we went through the multiple folders of files of photos of mum and dad all down the years.

It hurt to hear these words from dad in the midst of our family gathering. All of my time in the Dojo, all of my time in meditation, all of my time in therapy, all of my time in groupwork, all of my time in life, these were the resources I was able to call on in accepting and holding this shocking expression from dad.

12.08.20. The most immediate and physical difference I've noticed in myself since I began this daily practice of 'Mo(u)rning Pages' is that the coiled and roiling sensation of anxiety knotted in my stomach has dissipated almost to the point of being negligible or even absent on most mornings as I wake. More like I had a sense of low-level dissociation or fogginess about myself.

14.08.20. On our way to the fish & chip shop we took the 'scenic route' to get there. It was sweet and restorative to be on the beach. It seemed more important to me to just have a fluid and easy conversation as a way of re-establishing rapport and resonance together.

15.08.20. H had made it clear on Saturday night that she planned to travel back fairly early on Sunday morning. I climbed around and out to some of the boulders below the eastern side of the cove, simply to enjoy the water, the sun, the vista and the tranquillity.

16.08.20. It's been at least 12–18 months since I'd last been at L and B's place. Inevitably in the course of our conversation we talked through some of the details and process of their experience of managing the practical business surrounding these major losses to B's family.

17.08.20. It was with dad and F in mind that I awoke this

morning. The walk up to Dartington with L and B was relaxed. Over 2–3 hours it was grounding.

18.08.20. Whatever the actual psychological-emotional drivers are with L, what I realise this morning is that she has a raw intelligence. The walk around Dartington estate was very relaxing. It was enough to be responsive and present to what was arising between us, conversationally and energetically.

19.08.20. Dad relayed that rather than leaving early on Sunday morning, H had actually stayed until mid-afternoon. Until dad and L meet with the funeral directors we wouldn't know the actual date for the service.

20.08.20. When I left dad that Monday afternoon he was as well as we could have expected him to be. I'd arranged to meet S at the Docks in Exeter. S is an incredibly good artist.

21.08.20. We also have to consider, the ambitions and feelings that our young teenage son M has, in relation to his future and our wider family relations.

22.08.20. Dad is visiting H and F over the middle of this past week until next Monday. That first week of July was mostly 'fog'. I hope I will invest dive-time in further Constellations work to address these scars.

23.08.20. One of the aspects of this period of experience on learning about and following mum's dying has been feeling emotion. I'm wondering, though, at what point do I begin to feel a deeper more direct, raw emotional wave or tide?

24.08.20. It wasn't inevitable that I'd develop a 'do it and be damned' attitude to life. This seemed the most sensitive resolution of the matter. Relatively speaking we could relax together.

26.08.20. Yesterday I had a lengthy Zoom call with F. I brought us back home directly to mum and dad's place from the shop. Once we got back, we immediately set down to eating our fish & chip supper, sharing what we'd bought with dad.

27.08.20. Dad asked if I was sorry for the distress that I had caused to mum over the course of my life.

28.08.20. There was a kind of semi-detachedness in the flow of the conversations across our small family grouping. I hadn't seen mum since my last visit in mid-December 2019. For the first time I can remember, he was wearing his regimental tie.

29.08.20. Dad stepped forward and up to the lectern. Here was dad poetically declaring in a beautiful, steady, head-on and transparent way his undying love for mum. I felt so tender and raw in that moment.

30.08.20. Our family party gathered for around what seemed like 10–15 minutes or so in the assembly space under the awning outside of the crematorium chapel. There's a real sense of reassurance that dad will be looked out for by both E and L.

31.08.20. That evening of Thursday 16.07 was one of quiet reflection. What a strange, heart-warming, normal, surreal and rollercoaster episode. Mum finally gone.

01.09.20. I've had a number of conversations with close friends and colleagues about the loss of a parent in the months now since mum died. We are in the business of exploring the emotional entanglements that people experience in family life.

02.09.20. I miss mum. In their unplanned and unintended ways, mum and dad have been harbingers, the pioneers of a progressive dual-heritage family.

03.09.20. On the Friday morning 17.07 following mum's funeral service I was awake early. I think dad welcomed the opportunity to have some quiet reflective time to himself. Much laughter ensued.

04.09.20. In the afternoon passing the Halfway Inn I drove us up onto Dartmoor. I took my time in in both getting to and in climbing the Tor. I think we watched a bit of TV with dad later.

05.09.20. This is the first day I'm travelling out of London since Saturday 18.07. That's a full month and two weeks. It became evident in an instant that dad was still deeply raw, angry, wounded and lashing out in defence of his beloved. I offered the best warm and respectful, loving farewell I could muster in the circumstances – so, so strange.

06.09.20. The journey to the nearby petrol station was mostly in silence. Underlying this, though, was the deepening acceptance and coming to terms with the finality of mum being gone. Some life koan.

07.09.20. Today is the 33rd consecutive day that I have been writing these 'Mo(u)rning Pages' that relate directly to my thoughts, feelings, reflections, insights and spontaneous musings triggered by recalling the immediate events surrounding mum dying on 25.06 this year.

It was an emerging awareness. A dawning, a feeling. Somewhere around September 2020 there was a spike; it was during a phone call. A strangled, choking sound of distress. It was an instantly fearful scene. Something was wrong. A sense of loss of control. I was scared and shocked through and through. Hospitalisation was the outcome for my dad.

This moment was the beginning of a process. A gift. We set up a WhatsApp group family-wide. The outcome of the hospitalisation – a diagnosis of a Grade 4 inoperable tumour. The catalyst for hyper-awareness in my bones.

A childlike openness to his emotions. A directness in his expression of feelings and opinions. So candid and in the moment. Visceral. This shifted our relationship irreversibly. From being a remote and reserved man to becoming completely emotionally present. This was the gift – the offering in the moment of crisis and the remaking of our relationship.

Mum is a quilter. Now here we were quilting a new narrative of family dynamics.

I became engulfed in a sense of love. Here I was experiencing a tempest of feeling, a tantrum of unbridled spontaneous emotions. A kind of folding-in of all the parts of memory and feeling, from all down the years of my relationship with dad.

Dad was always a lover of nature. I gained my own appreciation of nature through him. He was a farmer at heart and an engineer by profession. He was a risk-taker and a fun-maker. There were never any rocks too big. There was never any ocean out of bounds to us as children. The times we spent together in nature, dad and us kids, were where our secret language of emotional depth and agility was fostered. This was the genesis of our physical attachment. Weaving connection. Weaving connection. Weaving connection.

It was the six-month anniversary of dad's passing back in January. A poignant and emotional moment of reflection for my siblings and me. I recalled holding hands with dad just after he had died.

This was a tidal shift. Tenderness and connection have become the predominant feelings that are present for me now.

An expansive appreciation. Integration. Self-acceptance. This is maturation. These are the precious gifts that have come from dad's final months and his passing. Precious, precious gifts.

7 Grief: Personal Stories from a Black Turkish Cypriot

Ertanch Hidayettin

Having qualified as a teacher in the late 1970s, Ertanch chose local government as a career. He worked in several community development and equality and diversity jobs for Haringey and Islington Council, and as an education consultant, delivering training courses for supplementary schools for the National Resource Centre for Supplementary Education for ten years, before retiring. He also served on various community sector organisations' management committees over the years, and acted as a coordinator for the Turkish Language, Culture and Education Consortium. He played a pivotal role in developing several Turkish-speaking community organisations. Ertanch writes for a number of publications aimed at the Turkish-speaking community, and has also presented weekly programs for Euro Genç TV.

The Oxford Dictionary definition of grief is: 'Intense sorrow, especially caused by someone's death.' This is my personal experience of grief as a Black British Turkish Cypriot.

Having arrived back home after a short holiday in Bournemouth in 2019 I received a call from my friend Ersoy, who was contacting me from his hospital bed. 'Come and see me as soon as possible. I haven't got much time', he said, with a hoarse voice. He had been in hospital for a few weeks and knew that he was not going to be leaving, so his two sons had arrived from Cyprus to see him one last time. His youngest had come to make peace because they had not been talking for a few months.

Ersoy and I had met only five years prior, and very soon we became close friends. He was a jovial, brilliantly entertaining friend. He was much older than me, with a very limited education, having barely completed primary education back in Cyprus, but he was a lot wiser than many of my university-educated friends. He joked that he had graduated from the University of Life, and I learned more from him than any biased history books. He was a true free spirit.

Having spent most of his childhood and youth in Cyprus, he knew a lot more than I did about the history of conflict in our beleaguered island. 'Abi' I called him – a title reserved for respected older brothers. Within a few hours of arriving home, I rushed to see him at the Royal Free Hospital in Hampstead, London. He was in a separate bedroom, barely conscious, but he opened his eyes and smiled sadly when he saw me. A few teardrops dribbled down from his left eye.

He could not talk, but his eyes did. When I asked him if he had any wishes, using his eyes and left hand he said he wished for his suffering to end.

A few days later he passed away with a sad smile on his lips not long after his two sons returned from a short respite holiday. His sons, two of his neighbours and I shed silent tears as the doctor came and examined him, certifying him dead.

Exactly three days later I would be witnessing another death – the death of my dear mother. She, too, had been in hospital for some time prior to her death. She had started dialysis treatment four years previously, and the orange Palliative Care End of Life Guidance that was issued each time she was admitted to hospital made us realise in no uncertain way that we were going to lose her in the not-so-distant future. Despite that, it was still a shock when one day the consultant who had been caring for her called my sister and I to her office and told us they were considering ending her treatment.

My dear, long-suffering mum finally died on the morning of 27th August 2019 on a sultry, hot morning during the early hours. It was 4:27 am. My older brother, who had arrived from Cyprus to be with her, my sister and I took turns to hold her hands as she was slipping away.

My friend Ersoy's death and my mum's death were expected. I was prepared for them, and no matter how heartbreakingly sad these awful occasions were, I had the necessary coping skills for them.

When I consider the pandemic that was to follow six-and-a-half months after they had gone, I think how timely their departures from this world were. There is no way they would have been able to cope with the horrible virus that was soon to come, and what is even worse is that they would have surely died lonely deaths with no one to hold their hands in their last hours. In my mum's case there would have been no imam to recite her favourite sections of the Quran to comfort her.

* * *

Even as a man of nearly 70, the two deaths on 24th and 27th August 2019 were the first times ever that I had witnessed people dying – people who were very close to me. Sure, I had been to many funerals of close relatives and friends. I was in London when my dad died in Cyprus, and because the dead must be buried within 24 hours in my family's religion, I was not able to get a ticket in time. Again, when my grandmother and aunt died in Turkey, I was not able to travel there in time. Another aunt had died in Germany, and I was only able to go there a few days after her death. These were my closest relatives who had died.

On reflection, my very first traumatic, close experience of death was when one of my cousins, Haluk, died at a very young age. I think it was a blood-related disease that brought about his untimely passing. We lived next to each other in my hometown, Lefka, Cyprus, where a lot of my relatives lived side by side in the same street with our orange grove overlooking their garden.

I remember one day all the children of my relatives were brought to our house and the adults were congregated at Haluk's house. We were secretly watching the proceedings from the holes in the garden wall and saw Haluk's small body laid out on a stone table as three women tenderly washed him. We were discovered and chased away. However, this scene stayed with me forever. Even now, I vividly remember the minutest details.

We lived opposite an old graveyard that had not been used in over a hundred years, and as children we had no qualms about playing in this place. We considered it an exciting adventure play-ground. We climbed on the huge cypress and walnut trees and an old olive tree that was over a hundred years old was our spaceship. We played there carefree during the long, hot summer days, but at nights we were scared to look out of our bedroom windows because they faced the graveyard. Such was the fear of death and dying we felt as children.

In my culture as a Turkish Cypriot it is very rare for children to attend funerals because of the belief that children must be protected from anything to do with death at all cost. 'Cost' is an appropriate word, as the mistaken intention to 'protect' children has dire consequences. It makes it so much more difficult and so much more traumatic when coming face to face with the only inevitable event in our lives.

* * *

Years later, the dreaded Covid-19 pandemic came, and is one of the most significant events in the recent history of humankind, claiming the lives of almost 7 million people worldwide. While the pandemic has subsided in 2023/24, its effects are still being felt around the whole. Like many people, it has personally affected me, too. It has affected me in an unimaginably cruel way.

My sister Asiye was a year younger than me, at 67. She was a large woman, my lovely sister. She was a diabetic but was managing to control her diabetes admirably by being careful about her diet. When Covid-19 came along she was very fearful of this new disease. Even before this deadly disease she would only go out of the house for essential reasons, such as visiting her GP or dentist, and shopping, because our mother's passing 15 months previously had left a very deep void in her life. She was our mother's carer and had looked after her in such a wonderfully caring, compassionate way, right up to her death. But after our mother had left this world, my sister became a changed woman. Her life was brightened a little when her son married; it gave her renewed purpose and she was over the moon when her new daughter-in-law arrived to live with them in the beginning of November 2020. Sadly, she only managed to enjoy her company for three weeks.

The Covid-19 test the whole family had taken two weeks before proved positive. My sister, brother-in-law, nephew and his newly arrived wife from Morocco all had the dreaded virus, but only my sister was affected very badly. She was not able to sleep, had frequent coughing fits, and her appetite disappeared completely. It was only because she was taking medication that she forced herself to eat. During those weeks large numbers of Covid-19 deaths were being reported, yet Asiye's death was still unexpected for us. It was a shock because we had not considered her particularly vulnerable.

On a cold November afternoon, 24th November 2020 to be exact, the phone rang. It was 3:30 pm, and as if I had a premonition, I looked at it in panic. I was not wrong. I was to receive unexpected, terrible news. My nephew on the other end of the line was crying uncontrollably, and I did not need to ask him what was wrong. I instinctively knew.

I experienced grief in so many different forms. At first, I felt an unbearable numbness at this shockingly unexpected event. I walked around in a daze, as if my senses had deserted me. I felt nothing. I am yet to get over this feeling, and looking back, I realise that I was showing clear signs of depression.

I once read a quote from Pastor Fran Buhler stating, 'Death is a friend – not something to dread and fear. In our sorrow, there is One we can trust. We may trust the Holy One. Death comes under His jurisdiction'.[1] But in contrast to what Pastor Fran Buhler says, death has never been considered a friend in my culture. Dread and fear, and of course extreme sorrow, are the most common feelings we experience when someone dies. In my Turkish Cypriot community grief is expressed very freely. Following death there is a lot of crying, with family and friends gathering, and communal praying at several special events.

Pastor Fran Buhler invites people to find solace in God at times of grief and many people do this, but not me, because I am not a religious person. It will not be an exaggeration to say that religion is not a major factor in the lives of the majority of Turkish Cypriots. My mother and sister were exceptions to this rule. They were devout Muslims, and both my parents had made the pilgrimage to Mecca, one of the five pillars of Islam. My sister was also hoping to do the same.

My mother became religious very late in her life, sometime in her early 60s, so my siblings and I were not brought up with much religion in our lives. However, almost everyone I knew fasted during Ramadan, although children were discouraged from doing so. We were only allowed to fast one day in the beginning, one day in the middle and on the last day of the Holy Month of Ramadan, so it was a novelty for us. We used to wait in anticipation in front of the mosque at the far corner of the graveyard. We waited there for the minaret lights to come on, which signified the end of fasting for the day, and then we would rush home and take our place at the dinner table, breaking our fast with an olive or a date. This, and being taken to visit one of the three mosques in our town, was the extent of our religious observance.

As children in primary school, we had a religious education lesson once a week, and I loved listening to the stories about Prophet Muhammad (pbuh) and his followers during these lessons. However, as a sign of defiance in the face of Islamophobia in recent years, when asked my religion I would state 'Muslim' and talk openly about Islam, even though I had no religious belief.

My sister's death had me wondering for the first time if being just a little bit religious would have helped me to grieve properly, and in that moment, I wished that I had some sort of religious belief.

Oh how I admire other cultures that honour and remember their loved ones after death, that celebrate their lives rather than mourn their deaths. Death, after all, is the only inevitable fact of life. The organising of a wake, music blaring and drinks gulped down in the home of the deceased or at a function hall is viewed with amazement in my culture, and the bringing of coffins to the home of the deceased is frowned upon. In short, death is one of those big taboo subjects.

***

As well as the tragedy of millions of lives lost, the pandemic also caused a very significant change – the suspension of the cultural, religious and social norms that human beings value. Whether or not we believe in a religion, when we are stripped of our culture and rituals, we become insignificant. We feel a huge sense of loss.

I strongly believe that 'a picture is worth a thousand words', and an iconic photograph showing my dear friend, Hüseyin Hodja, will always stay with me (Hodja literarily means 'teacher' and is used to describe schoolteachers as well as religious figures in Islam). In it, Hüseyin Hodja presides over a burial at the Islamic section of a graveyard in East London – just a solitary figure holding a see-through white umbrella to protect himself from the drizzling rain. The huge bucket of an orange-coloured digger performs the function of relatives attending the funeral. In our funerals it is an honour to shovel earth onto the coffin of the deceased following its lowering to the 6-feet deep grave. Men take turns to perform this last act of respect for loved ones. Using diggers is not acceptable.

Peter Nicholls, Reuters, 5 May 2020

The day of a funeral and for two consecutive days after, the family of the deceased organise prayer sessions attended by close family and friends, giving a great deal of comfort to the family. These communal displays of grief bind people together, and sometimes families will hire community centres for these important events.

This is repeated on the 40th day of death, and at this time, on just one occasion, family and friends of the deceased gather to pray.

Alas, the Covid-19 pandemic did not allow us to perform these religious and culturally important duties. These and other customs that help with the grieving process that were denied to us during the pandemic were replaced; funerals via Zoom became the norm. Were it not for the pandemic, my sister's funeral would have been attended by more than a hundred people, because she was very popular in the community. And, of course, in normal times my sister would not have been taken away from us so cruelly.

I do think about how I coped with my grief, and I know that I am yet to grieve properly. I feel guilty for the lack of tears, the tears that I have not shed for my beloved sister. I feel guilty for not trying enough to ensure she received the urgent treatment she needed, but on the other hand, I know people who were hospitalised and as a result lost their lives alone, without the comforting presence of loved ones.

I heard horrific stories, claims of people being treated differently by doctors, hospitals, ambulance crews and other health professionals on the grounds of their race. Don't ever believe that this disease treats everyone equally – that is a big lie.

I had felt anger towards my sister's family because I thought that one of them had given her this unwanted disease that caused her untimely death, but this anger did not last long because I soon realised the irrationality of my anger at them.

'Nothing is going to be the same after this', people say after a particularly traumatic event. I think this saying is very true for me. The loss of my sister, and the tragic circumstances surrounding her untimely, perhaps unnecessary, passing has meant that nothing will be the same anymore. The way I look at things has changed, the things I liked have changed too, things I considered important lost their appeal for me, they have become futile, meaningless.

I attended an online event held by the Ubele Initiative, an African diaspora-led organisation working to empower Black and racially minoritised communities in the UK, and found out about free grief counselling sessions on offer. The wonderful counsellor I spoke to on three occasions helped me. Prior to these sessions, I had not been able to bring myself to go into my sister's house to see the passageway where she had fallen and breathed her last breaths. Neither had I spoken to my brother-in-law, nephew and his wife about our common grief.

I eventually did all these things a few days before the house was sold, and on the day of the first anniversary of my sister's death, I went to the hill overlooking the house and looked towards it, imagining seeing her in the garden, tending to her beloved flowers and vegetables, and hanging out freshly laundered clothes on the line.

I also attended an Immersive Bereavement Training Workshop organised by the Ubele Initiative in April 2022, when we were introduced to the concept of 'ancestral veneration' and 'epigenetic inheritance' by the excellent Dalian Adofo, founder of Ancestral Voices,[2] an educational initiative dedicated to preserving and documenting African spiritual knowledge systems. It means our loved ones are not lost, and even though they may have died, their spirits are still within us. This, and many other things I learned from Dalian, was a big comfort to me, and I'd like to take this chance to express huge thanks to him and to the Ubele Initiative, and my deepest condolences for everyone who lost loved ones, either due to the coronavirus pandemic or for other reasons.[3]

Notes

1. Buhler, F. (2022) 'Heaven–faith is comforting.' Open to Hope, 6 May. www.opentohope.com/heaven-faith-is-comforting
2. https://ancestralvoices.co.uk
3. This article gives a very good description of how the Turkish Cypriot community was affected by the coronavirus pandemic: Grey, S. and Nicholls, P. (2020) 'In shielding its hospitals from COVID-19, Britain left many of the weakest exposed.' Reuters Investigates, 5 May. www.reuters.com/investigates/special-report/health-coronavirus-britain-elderly

8 Death Across Cultures: A Personal Reflection

Chukumeka Maxwell

Chukumeka was a probationary Christian Buddhist monk and assistant paramedic for four years each, and a Quaker chaplain for six years, as well as now being a suicide prevention facilitator, focusing on community development, mental health and wellbeing, social inequalities (cultural diversity) and social prescribing. He was the co-founding director and joint CEO of Action to Prevent Suicide CIC, and founder of the charity Goodwill In Action To Prevent Suicide CIO, Devon.

When I was originally asked to write a piece, I was somewhat arrogant, wanting to put across certain facts regarding death, dying and grief, but that changed when my ex-wife died recently, leaving me as a single father to a now 16-year-old girl, and then, just three weeks ago, the death of my ex-father-in-law. Suddenly all day-to-day existence seems futile, and yet it is so important to continue because there is always life beyond death.

This is a personal reflection incorporating my lived experiences of Black grief, loss and bereavement, and my hope for and understanding of good practice. Although grief and loss are universal, there are differences in the way individuals and communities experience and express them. Race, culture, ethnicity and faith all play a part.

In my lifetime I have had various roles that are particularly relevant to experiences of grief and loss. I was a child in a civil war and then living in an area of London known as the 'Murder Mile'.[1] I was a probationary Christian Buddhist monk, an assistant paramedic and first responder, a Quaker prison chaplain, a social worker, an associate university lecturer, a family support worker, a community development mental health worker, a mental health mentor, and the founder of a suicide prevention organisation. My reflections on grief are influenced by all those variables, and by my Black British identity.

I am from three main ethnic heritage and cultural identities. My father was Nigerian from what was called the Ibo tribe of Biafra near Port Harcourt, Nigeria, now known as the Ikwerre/ Rivers State people. My mother was Jamaican from the parish of Manchester in an area called Knockpatrick, some 50 miles from the capital Kingston. I was born in Hackney, London and have lived in three countries – Nigeria in 1965–67 during the civil war, before I was evacuated back to the UK in 1967, then Jamaica 1971–74, with a short interlude in Belize (formerly known as British Honduras). Apart from travelling to a few other countries, I have spent most of my life predominantly in the UK – in East London, Kent, Suffolk, Sussex, Somerset, Berkshire, and now Devon for the last 18 years.

Being seen as a racial minority wherever I have lived has led me to inhabit varying cultures, cults and tribes, and within each I have witnessed many deaths; through those diverse experiences I have gained a personal and universal understanding of death.

My view and experiences of death across these cultures caused a numbing of my senses as a protective mechanism. I did not grieve, which resulted in a profound loneliness that manifested in suppressing unresolved emotions. Joy and sadness are my heart responses, and if the heart is not exercised in a healthy way, it creates dis-ease. Holding in that grief also affected my physical health, and I believe it is responsible for me being diagnosed with liver problems and bladder cancer.

There are three distinct episodes that exacerbated these issues. The first was being stuck in the middle of Yoruba, Lagos, in 1966, when people were being arrested in front of me at gunpoint and marched off and shot in the distance. I could hear the shots of the anti-aircraft guns going all night and people being shot down and falling from the sky. If you read or watch films, I'd recommend *Half of a Yellow Sun* by Nigerian author Chimamanda Ngozi Adichie, published in 2006, which tells the story of the Biafran War through the perspective of the characters. Both the film and the audiobook rekindled memories in me, resulting in bodily sensations that were long forgotten.

Our own family story was also featured in a book called *Betwixt Heaven and Charing Cross: The Story of St Martin-in-the-Fields* by Carolyn Scott, published in 1971. In one chapter my name is John, and the author writes, 'I don't think my children will ever get over what they saw. John was just gone 5. He still cries a lot, and he is only 8 now but his hair has begun to go grey.'

I highlight these incidents to show you, the reader, how my inability to grieve, or too much grief, has manifested into an imbalance of my physical and emotional health. For this reason, I urge practitioners to ask the correct questions, following intuition and wisdom and not perceived knowledge.

Grieving is natural! I now consider my inability to grieve an adverse childhood experience tied closely to the hypothesis of 'post-traumatic slavery syndrome'. This has been described by psychiatrist Alvin Francis Poussaint, journalist Amy L. Alexander, Joy DeGruy and by Bessel van der Kolk in his bestselling book *The Body Keeps the Score*, and I have witnessed it.

Two of my friends from that time died by suicide and another is institutionalised in a psychiatric unit. So how, then, do we begin to answer the conundrum of grief and loss in the Black community and the inequalities and injustices that the community continues to endure?

A friend said that when it comes to grief 'we cannot breathe' – a reflection on the death of George Floyd in the USA in May 2020, which sparked an outpouring of rage, grief and shock. But we all need to breathe – that is life.

I learned not to express grief because of my sensitivity, bullying at boarding school and internalised and externalised racism.

When my Nigerian grandmother died, I was shocked and confused, whereas my father, a member of the Commonwealth Judiciary who I would describe as being 'more English than the English themselves', wailed and ripped his shirt and beat the floor furiously. This expression of grief was so alien to me. It was one of the two times I saw my father's grief expressed, but he very quickly reverted to his stiff upper lip.

I believe that practitioners should be comfortable with not knowing, and be open to intuition and wisdom, rather than the 'knowledge of knowing' that changes and evolves over time.

The diversity of the impact of grief is not necessarily linked to illness, but when I was recently bereaved, I was diagnosed with acute stress. I'm not proposing that we should see bereavement as an illness; however, the environmental factors of bereavement had an overwhelming response for me on an emotional and physical level as well as mental manifestations.

I was fortunate to receive finance and goodwill from my workplace, which has meant that I have been able to face my sadness, joy and many other emotions without being held hostage by an unsympathetic employer. As a health and wellbeing coach, my job requires a degree of authenticity in my emotions to create a relationship with people I am trying to work with and serve. I have been struck by the waves of spontaneous rising of grief and the ability for it to pass very quickly, and by the level of kindness and the outpouring of support. Inwardly, I feel a degree of stubbornness and don't accept help that has been offered, but this, too, could be part of the reality of not expressing grief.

One thing we can be certain of is that we are all going to die, and it is my belief, in keeping with many traditions, that we all are going to reincarnate. But what does a good death look like, and how can we grieve and continue to thrive and not just survive? One day my Jamaican grandmother said that she could hear angels, so my aunt told her to go and lay down, and when she did, she fell into a deathly sleep. Is that considered a good death?

I often challenge interpretations of death that do not speak of reincarnation because I believe it makes death and suffering harder to cope with. The idea that as Black people 'we can't grieve' has weight for me due to the survival mechanism of numbing sadness and grief that some of us develop. Such mechanisms can also numb joy and gratitude. Grief is a sense of acknowledgement, and when it is numbed it affects the ability to properly celebrate a person's life. It is through good deeds and kindness and working under the law of love that I believe one reincarnates to serve humanity, so acknowledgement is important. This way of thinking is propagated in many aboriginal cultures and is also deep within Tibetan Buddhism, but it can be hard for those in Western societies to conceptualise, and that includes grief counsellors.

Years ago, I had the honour and privilege to witness my mother dying in a hospice. She wanted her body to be used for medical science, but due to the nature of her death, her request was turned down. This meant that we had to change our plans and organise for her cremation and interment next to my deceased father, and that impacted my grief.

I do think that the fixed ideas about the process of grief – like 'the grief curve' – create a linear view of how an individual may grieve, and is an example of Deus ex machina, or 'God in the machine', convincing ourselves of a convenient resolution, but one that I think is actually counterintuitive and against our natural response. When you think about it, even in the animal kingdom, when elephants lose one of their herd they grieve, as do apes. So why should humans feel constrained from expressing their natural grief knowing it can create other health challenges?

In the UK, many of the cultural concepts of death that are traditionally practised in Africa and the Caribbean have been diminished in favour of clinical approaches rooted in Western medicine and psychiatry. I was recently in hospital with a person at the end of life, and within an hour of them dying we were asked to clear their room and leave the hospital. Even though it wasn't meant to be a cold, calculated move, it did not allow us the time and space to grieve. Traditionally, we would have been able to sit quietly with the body and express our grief, which is not necessarily a sad thing to do.

Death is real and we cannot avoid it in our personal, professional and cultural lives, but when it does occur it can cause mental and emotional as well as physical reactions. It can produce tears – an immense amount of tears which can sometimes make us feel like we are drowning. But there is life beyond death. Life continues for those of us who are left behind and who grieve the death of those who have died.

The way that we react to grief also changes over time, often coming in waves. Even though we cannot stop the waves, we can learn to surf them.

It is also possible to use grief as a catalyst for change – to use the death of one thing as the time to birth something else. For example, I am resolute in using the most recent death and the past losses as a mechanism for deepening my spiritual practice so that I can grieve and live in Joy.

For some, when they are grieving it becomes the first time that they take the step to engage with a therapist or grief practitioner. But no matter the modality or role that the practitioner plays, it is not so much about the theory but that the person who is grieving is supported so that they can heal. The quality of the relationship – a human placebo – which enables the person to heal themself – is important. It enables healing to take place on a spiritual level, which, depending on that person's culture, may involve Light, God, the energy of the avatar or Jesus. What matters is that the intensity and the devotion of a person's spiritual belief is not negated.

The Black African and Caribbean community faces a significant amount of discrimination, racism and prejudice. As a community we have endured immense suffering, and sometimes that makes it difficult to contextualise how we grieve and what we are grieving for. When we are forced to factor forgiveness into our grief, it can be the hardest thing to do, but we know that it helps with the grief process. Forgiveness helps us to become tender in our heart, and open to what in Tibetan Buddhism is referred to as 'the petals of the Lotus' in our heart.

The loved ones I have lost are still within my heart, and so when I do grieve I also celebrate and love them all over again.

Notes

1. Brinkhurst-Cuff, C. (2016) 'Does "Murder Mile" still deserve its name?' *Hackney Post*, 15 March. http://hackneypost.co.uk/murder-mile

Shed a Tear

Amanda Inniss

Men are told they should not cry
I don't know why, I do not know why?
Are their eyes not linked to their soul?
Do they not feel the bitter bite of grief?
When grief bites, she bites with an iron jaw.
She is cold and she is harsh
Her sharp teeth easily ruin's the flesh of the mightiest of men.
No, men should not cry
For they are instructed to stand tall
As tall as an oak
To face the cruel wind of grief without movement
Without a shudder
Or a lesser man they will be.
Do not be void of emotion
Unable to see or reach that inner river,
Till it swells and surges
Breaking its banks with nowhere to flow.
Cry
Shed a tear to feel
Shed a tear and heal
Shed a tear to get through this time
And if you need to,
Shed a tear and
Cry Cry.

9 Black Queer Grief

Dennis Carney

Dennis[1] is chair of Black Connection, a UK-wide social network for Black queer men aged 50+ formed in response to the Covid-19 pandemic. He has appeared in the Channel 4 documentaries Black OUT, Trainers Reggae and the Olympics and Under Your Nose. Dennis lives in Brixton, South London, and in 2003 and 2006 he received Black LGBT Community Awards recognising his contributions in raising the profile of Black Queer communities in the UK.

I was born in Manchester back in 1962, and still can't quite believe that I celebrated my 60th birthday earlier this year. I'm the first-born of four kids to Jamaican parents who moved to the UK in the late 1950s. I moved from Manchester to London when I was 20 years old to 'come out' as a Black gay man because I didn't feel confident enough to be 'out' in Manchester back then.

Since moving to London 40 years ago I've been very active in the Black Queer community. I was chair of the Black Lesbian and Gay Centre (BLGC) project for about five years in the mid-1980s, and chair of Stonewall Housing Association and the Black Gay Men's Advisory Group in the 1990s. I worked at PACE, an LGBT mental health charity, for 12 years, and set up a monthly support group for Black gay men there. I was also involved in successfully negotiating the Reggae Compassionate Act, which put an end to Jamaican dancehall 'Murder Music' being sold and distributed or performed around the world, ending this extremely harmful period in Reggae music history. I established a grass-roots organisation called Black Connections, the UK's first social network for Black queer men aged 50+.

I know this is not the case for a lot of other Black queer men due to homophobia and stigma around the idea of homosexuality in Black and Brown communities. Considering this, I feel particularly blessed to have the love and support of my extended family since 'coming out' in 1982. They have always been there for me.

I also feel really proud to have been awarded two Black LGBT Community Awards for my community development work with Black LGBT communities in 2003 and 2006, and I feel honoured to have recently appeared in two TV documentaries – *Positive* (Sky TV) and *Moments that Shaped: Queer Black Britain* (BET UK) – so over the years I've become a very visible member of the QTIPOC (Queer, Transgender and Intersex People of Colour) community here in London.

The earliest memory I have of grief and loss was finding out that my first boyfriend from back when I lived in Manchester took his life in his mid-20s. I was devastated, and remember thinking that homophobia was the main reason behind his suicide, as he suffered a lot of hatred from his family and local community because of his sexuality.

In 1982, shortly after moving to London, I began to hear stories about the 'gay plague' – which was the beginning of the HIV epidemic. I remember thinking, 'I don't have to worry about HIV too much because I'm in a relationship, and all the images I see of people living with HIV are White gay men, so I'm safe.' However, by the end of the 1980s, I learned that my first gay partner who I had lived with when I initially moved to London had died from an AIDS-related condition.

I've also lost way too many close friends to the disease. In fact, I was by the bedside of one of my best friends when he died. HIV caused the deaths of many brilliant Black queer men whose lives were cut too short. It had a devastating impact world-wide, and yet the Black Queer community was largely invisible when it came to addressing the specific cultural needs of this underserved community.

Like many others, the thing about grief in those days, especially around HIV, was that I didn't feel I could talk freely about it. The kind of support services we have today when dealing with traumatic life events simply didn't exist, and given the invisibility of the Black Gay community, very little mental health and wellbeing support was available. I recall several Black gay men died isolated and alone, often ostracised by family and friends – in most instances due to the fear, shame and stigma associated with HIV/AIDS.

In the 1980s and 1990s there was a lot of stigma, and even now there's still some stigma around HIV. I think that has made it really difficult for the Black Queer community to find spaces to talk about the impact it has on their lives. The only people I could really talk to about it were my friends, and this was not always easy, as they were also dealing with multiple losses themselves.

Around that time I was invited to join the management com-mittee of Big Up, a Black Queer-led and run, HIV voluntary or-ganisation that provided HIV prevention initiatives targeting Black gay and bi men. Because of that I had other Black queer men I could talk to who understood and who were also committed to getting accurate, lifesaving HIV prevention information for our community out there. However, despite this, I still feel like I've been carrying for many, many, many years the impact of all those multiple bereavements. I avoid attending funerals when I can as I find them too emotionally challenging to handle as they often bring up many painful memories for me. I think that's added to the pile of grief I've had to deal with throughout my adult life.

One way I dealt with grief after attending countless funerals was to avoid them, but the downside of this was that I didn't allow myself the opportunity to share my grief with others and publicly pay my respects. Instead, I carried it silently in a lot of ways. Looking back, my earliest memory of grief was losing my first boyfriend to suicide and then my second to HIV, another partner died from HIV, and another was diagnosed as HIV positive while we were together. I've lost count of how many friends and people I know who lost their lives and loved ones to this devastating disease.

In fact, representation of Black men was practically non-existent in terms of HIV prevention materials – for example, the Terrence Higgins Trust weren't putting out materials with Black or Brown gay men on the front cover. So, for a long time, in the early days of the epidemic, I didn't really worry about HIV because I thought it only affected White gay men because all the images that I ever saw in connection with HIV were White gay men. I thought, 'Oh, well, I'm not White, so I don't have to worry about it.'

In addition to this, If I was lucky enough to see a Black man in any gay press or magazines at this time, he would normally have his usually muscular arms wrapped around a White guy or be semi-naked in an advert selling sex or wearing a dress, high heels, make-up and a wig. Nothing wrong with Black men doing any of this, of course, and I notice not too much has changed today when it comes to the 'hyper'-sexualisation and racist stereotyping of Black men particularly within the Gay community. Pick up any gay magazine today, read it, and tell me I'm wrong!

I also remember that for a lot of family members and friends, for many at a funeral this would be the first time that they learned their deceased relative was gay or had been living with HIV – that's if anyone was brave enough to reveal these often-hidden facts and secrets.

With every cloud there's a silver lining in my book, in that many in the Black Queer community and their allies came together to help and support those who were affected by HIV. We looked after each other because nobody else was looking after us. A good example of this was the creation of Big Up.

I think that one positive outcome from the HIV epidemic was, in some ways, to galvanise the community into action in a way that I don't think was there prior to the epidemic. Because so many of us were dying, we had to do something, and certainly for me I didn't want other Black gay men to die. That motivated me to get the information out there and to try to do what I could to help stop the deaths of Black gay men.

I remember going to Bootylicious, a Black gay club, and we took two sets of HIV information leaflets and pamphlets to hand out. We had one with a Black guy on the front cover and another one with a White guy on the front cover and we piled them up next to each other, and every single one of the pamphlets with the Black guy on the front went and not one with the White guy on the front got taken. Representation matters!

The Covid-19 pandemic really brought back lots and lots of painful memories and connections to the early days of the HIV epidemic. In terms of my own family, I think I've been very lucky that none of my family members have died from Covid-19. However, I've lost count of how many people I know who lost relatives during the Covid-19 pandemic. I know of one friend who lost three relatives in the space of two weeks in the first wave.

Again, there had been very, very few spaces where people from Black or Brown communities could easily get support around dealing with their grief due to the Covid-19 pandemic, and it feels very similar, if not identical, to the kind of experience I had during the HIV epidemic. I found attending funerals really difficult, so I didn't go to a single funeral during the pandemic, yet I lost lots and lots of people I know. The trauma is just too challenging, especially because I have some guilt about surviving, with that recurring nagging question at the back of my mind, 'Why them and not me?'

Therapy helps. Being able to talk about it with my friends has helped, and one thing that definitely helped was that the Ubele Initiative commissioned a series of workshops aimed at Black queer men to look at grief and its impact in terms of our community. Those were really valuable spaces in terms of getting support and sharing. In fact, they were invaluable, especially for the men who attended them, and it's been helpful to talk about this in therapy. But, of course, therapy is not accessible to a lot of Black people. It's expensive, and there's this cultural norm that exists within our community around privacy. I can remember my mother telling me growing up as a kid, 'No bother put your business on the street'. The message was loud and clear– don't tell your business to others. She was saying this to protect me as a young Black man in the 1960s and 1970s growing up on a council estate with often hostile, racist neighbours. So I understand her message.

For many years I saw therapy as a 'White person's thing', but that belief was a bit ludicrous because if we look back to our past histories, before colonialism and slavery, there were shamans within our communities we could talk to. The philosophy of 'Each one teach one', 'It takes a village to raise a child', and that 'The village looks after everybody' is the same as therapy in a lot of ways. Even our Black churches have been great sources of support, especially in terms of dealing with grief, and when you think about cultural rituals such as 'Nine Night celebrations', where the life of the person who has passed is celebrated, it is evident that talking and sharing helps with grief. But during the HIV epidemic, because of the stigma attached to HIV, many people didn't have the traditional Nine Night celebrations of the person's life.

The reality for a lot of Black people during the Covid-19 pandemic is that they've been dealing with grief alone, and it is not because Black people want to do that. It is because society as a whole had to deal with not being able to attend funerals and grieve in the way that is their cultural tradition. That had a real impact on our community, and we have not really talked about it enough. So many people just had to deal with it, including myself, and develop our own coping mechanisms. That's another reason why those workshops were valuable spaces in terms of getting support and spaces to talk about the impact of grief in Black Queer communities.

My mother always told me, 'If it doesn't kill you, it makes you stronger', and whenever I think about that saying, I think about my mum. She's 81, and I know that she's not going to be around forever, and I often think about how I am going to deal with it. A few of my friends have lost their parents recently, and I've seen the impact that has had on them, so I worry about how I'm going to manage and cope. One thing that does help me is remembering that I've been dealing with grief for most of my adult life. When I hear myself say that, it gives me strength and hope that I will survive it, and I hope that I will manage as I have done for the last 40 years.

My sister's partner died during the pandemic after they were together for 15 years, and that had really impacted me in a way that I had not anticipated. I wish I'd told him how much I valued the love that he gave to my sister, because for my sister, he was the love of her life. Prior to his death it wasn't something that was foremost in my thinking, and I feel a huge amount of guilt. The lesson I have learned is to tell the people I love and care for that I love and care about them.

Notes

1. https://dennislcarney.com

10 Widowed and Young: Condolences, Rallying and Drying Out

Tolulope Olajide

Tolu is a dedicated father of two, and after a profound personal loss, he used his expertise in transforming processes and optimising operations to establish Balanced Wheel,[1] a bereavement support charity. Tolu's own journey through grief has enriched his empathetic leadership style, with a keen emphasis on mental and emotional wellbeing alongside productivity. His operational excellence has driven change within his charity, enabling a swift and efficient response to those needing bereavement support.

I am no stranger to death. I had experienced the deaths of older family members and others who were 2 degrees away from my social network. I had taken part in the mourning rituals surrounding these losses, been to a few funerals, and never thought much of what happens next to the bereaved individual or families after their funerals. I rarely followed up or checked in on the bereaved after the funeral, and assumed that burying a loved one was the end of grief.

This experience changed slightly when sadly, in 2008, my older brother, who was in his mid-20s, lost a three-year battle to cancer. Again, I witnessed the mourning rites. We mourned his death, planned and did his funeral. As a family, we rarely spoke about our grief. It appeared that no one spoke about him again after the funeral. Our social network and the faith community around us appeared mute about grief and the riotous conflicting journey through grief. We returned to our workplaces where the only support was the three bereavement leave days offered, and somehow, life was to continue.

Significant rhetoric from my faith community suggested that we accept death, surrender to God's sovereignty by not asking questions, and accept the religious clichés. The cultural communities encouraged and reinforced stoicism and masculine grief through their passionate rhetoric. I later found that this script of internalising grief, appearing stoic and masculine, was not unique to my grief experience. It's been a script that has been played and passed down from generation to generation. Conversations about death, dying and bereavement appeared to be taboo, a conversation you rushed and swept under the carpet as quickly as you could.

It is these experiences that informed my understanding and belief. Unfortunately, I believed and adopted the inherited approach and attitude to grief and bereavement. I suppressed any uncomfortable emotions I felt, rarely let anyone into my emotional space, and carried on with life. I now saw grief and bereavement through the lens of 'silver lining thinking', and I was emotionally unavailable to other people's grief, unconsciously distancing myself from anyone who experienced it, rationalising their grief and comparing their expression with mine. It was difficult for me to empathise with anyone bereaved.

That attitude and belief was about to change when I experienced my most significant loss to date. My wife, Chidinma Onuzo, fell briefly ill towards the end of March 2020. She was admitted into hospital, and six days later, on the morning of 30th March 2020, I received the dreaded call no one wants to hear about their loved one, informing me of my wife's death. That news thrust me forcefully onto the path of being a young and widowed parent who was now the primary carer for our five-month-old baby and two-year-old toddler. I felt my life, represented by a glass cup, had been hit by a fast-moving train, shattering into many pieces.

What I share here is a combination of my lived experience and that of others, supported by research on life after the loss of a loved one. I have included lessons learned, I challenge assumptions and I offer suggestions, especially to the social networks.

In the hours and days that followed my wife's death, the recurring questions on my mind were: what's next? Will I survive this? Who will help me? And where can I get help? When I go to a new place, for example to a meeting or a conference, one of the first things I look for is finding someone like me. I found this to be true also for my grief journey.

The referral pathway for the African diaspora and other racially minoritised communities on bereavement, grief and loss is near non-existent, and if there is any, it lacks visibility. While the hospital provided me with a leaflet about the next step, namely registering the death, outside of that I found the information pack of little use.

In the acute phase of my grief, I found changes in my mental health. I experienced depression, guilt, fear, envy, anxiety, anger and loneliness as I withdrew myself socially and isolated from others. I became mainly preoccupied with thoughts of my wife, feelings of helplessness, hopelessness and self-reproach, and my self-esteem was very low. I was physically fatigued and agitated, and I cried a lot.

My social circle did their best to support me, primarily through the early phase of my grief providing practical support, administrative support and a listening ear. But two key questions that remain residing in my heart are: how is the social network of the bereaved managing their grief? And who supports the social network of the bereaved so that they do not become compassionately fatigued?

The social support I received was in three phases, namely 'condolences', 'rallying' and 'drying out'.

In the condolences phase people had good intentions, but they sometimes said or did things that hurt me as a bereaved person. Most people don't go out of their way to be hurtful or be insensitive, and the condolences and words of comfort that went well with me were from those who were authentic, but I found that a significant number of condolences were robotic, scripted and passively-aggressively wanted me to bend to their religious or cultural views, and most of what was said I deemed to be unhelpful.

After that came the rallying phase and it is true to say that most African diaspora communities still maintain a sense of community. Acquaintances, friends and families celebrated with the celebrant, and I know that the communities that my wife and I and family belong to would often raise collections to help families cushion the financial blow caused by the death of their loved one, such as funeral costs etc.

I received many well intentioned but overwhelming volumes of telephone calls, messages and sometimes home visits, especially in the early phase of the grief journey. But I observed that the number of people that reached out to check in on me or offer support dropped significantly after the funeral, and in that drying out phase the support had fallen off the cliff at the time when I felt I needed it the most. The funeral planning distracted my grief, but after the funeral was over, I found the silence of loneliness deafening, insomnia was steady, and the conflicting cocktail of grief was ravaging.

Beyond the funeral, I found that most people in my faith community appeared to be underprepared to help me, and my social network didn't know how to help me either. I was desperate for information so that I could understand what I was experiencing and to connect with others who may have journeyed on this grief path I now found myself on. I detested my new status of 'widower' and 'widowed parent'. I felt stigmatised. Even though my closest support network didn't act or behave in a way to make me feel stigmatised, I still longed to connect with someone who had been on a similar journey. I longed to connect with someone who sounded and looked like me; my longing wasn't to compare notes but perhaps to find a safe space and help validate some conflicting thoughts and emotions.

There is indeed no correct way to grieve, and in my grief journey so far I have observed that subcultures within the African diaspora communities tend to process and express their grief differently. For example, I belong to the millennial generation, and my default state is to question what I don't understand and pursue information until I am satisfied with my level of knowledge – whereas I think that most first- and second-generation migrants will tend to accept the things they don't understand, believing that it will make sense someday. So you can imagine the tension that arises when someone with a first- or second-generation belief and attitude to grief attempts to console me through their lens, and it appears that they're not getting to me. The result is frustration on both sides; they then withdraw and further distance themselves, sending me into deeper depths of loneliness and social isolation.

Seeing that I was fast becoming a shadow of myself, my concerned social network recommended that I consider bereavement counselling, and a friend checked to find out if Cruse Bereavement Support[2] could help me. We found out that the demand for Cruse's service was high, and I was informed that it would take six weeks before I could receive support. Six weeks felt like forever; I needed immediate information, and as I was struggling with sleeplessness in my grief, I searched the internet and social media for help and found three mainstream organisations in the UK that claimed to support those who were widowed and young. I remember reading through their websites and thought, 'I can't find anyone who looks like me so how will they be able to help me?'

My curiosity got the best of me as I found myself reading their Charity Commission's reports to see how diverse they were. I desperately wanted to find information and content created by someone who looked or sounded like me because there are some nuances that someone of the same heritage will quickly grasp without me having to explain further or give background context. The more I searched, the more I noticed the scarce bereavement support from the lens of the African diaspora. I unearthed a lack of diversity in the voices that dominated the bereavement spaces, whether in informational blogging, academic research, spiritual, social support etc. Grief research, narratives and support programmes had very limited information pertinent to African diaspora communities, and I discovered that more than 95 per cent of books, information, videos around bereavement, grief and were written by people who were not from the African diaspora or other racially minoritised communities. Having said that, I do, however, commend the tremendous effort put into the body of grief work, and I did find great value in identifying and expressing my grief through their content.

The central question in my mind at the time was, is the limited bereavement information and support from the African diaspora a function of availability or visibility? Then I stumbled across a report written in 2017 by the National Bereavement Alliance, suggesting that 55 per cent of bereaved people do not accept support.[3]

I retorted at my laptop screen as I read the report that 'I bet the majority of that 55 per cent is made up people from the African diaspora and other racially minoritised communities, and I wonder why?' The report further highlighted that of the 45 per cent who will accept support of some kind, 30 per cent will accept counselling from trained and supervised volunteer bereavement support workers, and 9 per cent will accept therapeutic counselling from specialist bereavement counsellors.

The report proposes that for most bereaved individuals their inner resources, family and friends will support their distress and subsequent adjustments to their losses, and that approximately a third need non-specialist, informal support, with only a small proportion being at risk of developing 'complicated grief', which is characterised by intense grief that can last for a more extended period compared with social expectations or cause impairment in daily functioning. My understanding of that framework was that the social network of the bereaved plays a crucial role in their grieving process, and so I liken the pathway to playing a game and excelling through the levels, except that you move to the next level if the player (the bereaved individual) fails the previous level.

I must admit that I was enjoying reading and learning as I was trying to make sense of my own grief, but I found myself unfamiliar with some of the terminology used around losing a loved one, which was a significant barrier point for me. It meant that I was still wanting information, resources and voices representing my own grief experiences to glean from and validate my experience.

That got me thinking and asking more questions. Is it that we have to pretend that people from African diaspora communities do not lose loved ones, and why is it that we shy away from sharing this vulnerable moment of our lives – does it mean that we automatically heal after the funeral of our loved one?

There is such limited content around life after loss from the perspective of the African diaspora communities that I wondered where the articles, books, podcasts, research and voices of people who have been underrepresented in grief support are. Is it that there are existing pockets of content from the African diaspora communities on grief and it's a matter of visibility and access to the contents that have been created, or could it be that the limited terminology used by the communities in their content makes it difficult to find? I also believe that many of the resources I've discovered deserve a wider audience.

Six months into my grief, I decided to share my journey as a legacy to my wife's memory and to try to make sense of my grief, loss and bereavement as I adjust to my new life as a young and widowed parent. I decided to start Balanced Wheel – initially as a platform where I would share my honest experience as a young Black widowed father navigating my new normal as a single parent and everything else in between through blog posts, videos, and eventually, as a community. My hope was that in sharing my stories they would serve as lived experience resources for people who may have lost their loved one and need help making sense of and coping with their grief. I also hoped to build a vibrant community where the bereaved and their social support network (individuals, friends, families and communities) could find healing, sustain hope, rebuild, rebalance and thrive as they journey together through grief.

I wasn't sure if anyone was paying attention to the stories I shared until I began to read the comments, and a couple of months later, three other people who had also lost a loved one but who were not in my social circle reached out to share their journey. While their loss was different from mine, I felt connected to them through our shared grief, and they felt liberated to have their experiences validated. That resurfaced questions that have remained persistent in my grief journey – is it that we have to pretend that people from African diaspora communities do not lose loved ones, and why do we shy away from sharing this vulnerable moment of our lives? What could life after the loss of social support look like?

Most of the mainstream bereavement support I found is geared towards emotional and informational support. Not that there's anything wrong with this type of support, but I think that a bereaved person from the African diaspora community may find it easier to engage and receive support if they know that they are also going to be helped to identify and navigate the other areas of their lives affected by grief. When that is added to the socio-economic disadvantage that many of us in the African diaspora find ourselves in, it means that we have no choice but to 'be strong', otherwise bills will be piling up and chores will be left undone etc. One of the common questions I have come across is, 'So how does this emotional stuff help me pay the bills and lighten my financial burden?'

Myself, and others around me, have also wondered how we, as bereaved individuals, are supposed to reintegrate. Often the focus is on the primary loss and the secondary losses are overlooked. I do wonder what bereavement support would look like if instrumental and informational social support were the lead actors in the services offered.

Can you imagine how useful it would be to help someone with their secondary loss regularly through a befriending service, for example, a chore like mowing their garden, which focuses on the task and not the individual? I reckon that as the main task is being carried out conversations will arise that could begin to allow the bereaved to put words to their emotions, gradually bringing them out of loneliness and social inaction.

African diaspora communities are historically resistant to counselling and therapy mainly because of the stigma attached to mental health. We are also afraid of the quality of the services we will receive, and unsure that we will get the right support if a crisis happens, so we tend to brace ourselves and we are stoic.

When I think about the impact of the enslavement of people from the African continent that ended in the not too distant past and the rampant racism experienced by generations of migrants, it is easy to extrapolate the rationale behind the resistance to receiving bereavement support from the mainstream. It is understandable why, as someone from the African diaspora, I dislike being vulnerable. How can I trust the system when I am unsure that the information received and kept about me won't be used against me or my children in the future? That fear runs deep. There is generally a high level of suspicion of professionals from outside of the community because even when help is sought, there's a likelihood that information is withheld, so I don't always trust that the providers have my best interests at heart.

The ongoing complex challenges experienced by the African diaspora communities due to enslavement, racism overtones, restricted access and privilege validate our emotional responses to significant life events such as the death of a loved one. This then causes our default grief response to often be guarded; we suppress our emotions, and sometimes portray an outward appearance of false resilience. Some people also struggle with limited emotional language, which can make it difficult to truly communicate feelings.[4] When asked the question 'How are you?', a likely response will often be 'I am good/all right/okay', which is more common in the first- and second-generation migrant community than third-generation migrants.

Based on my experience, I think that the level of openness and willingness to receive support is determined by level of trust and where the bereaved individual is in terms of their needs. I believe that the primary need for most bereaved individuals from the African diaspora is safety and security.

The stories I was sharing on the Balanced Wheel connected with other social circles outside mine, and it began to give the bereaved and their social networks validation and space to start a dialogue about grief, bereavement and loss – so much so that five months after starting the blog we held our first peer support group with a regular attendance of 13 widowed young people over a period of five months. I also noticed that based on the hundreds of conversations I have had with bereaved individuals, their social network, community and faith leaders from the African diaspora, the socio-economic needs of the bereaved is a consistent theme that has emerged.

On the eve of Christmas 2021 I stumbled across a review paper that clearly articulated what was in my heart, so you can imagine my excitement. It communicated what I had been penning in my journal for 17 months – titled 'Bereavement care for ethnic minority communities: A systematic review of access to, outcomes from, and satisfaction with, service provision',[5] it reinforced and validated my thoughts on the importance of equipping social networks with the right toolbox and skills so that they can effectively support their bereaved loved ones.

The paper synthesised the existing evidence on bereavement care by addressing questions on the barriers to accessing bereavement care for people from minority ethnic populations; the outcomes and satisfaction levels for those accessing the services; and what models of care provision exist to address the specific needs of the population. It also spoke of the importance of contextualising the information to various communities so that 'compassionate communities' can emerge with the right skills, information and knowledge to support people through any of the 40 life events that trigger grief. Those were the very things that I had been mulling over and writing about.

Sharing my grief experience through a diary and informational style of blogging has been extremely challenging, but I am glad I took the step to start the journey. The audience responses have provided me with social support through their validation, compliments, encouragement, knowledge sharing and companionship through online and offline feedback. For me it has been a win-win and has contributed to helping me get a sense of balance, and has also helped thousands of bereaved individuals and their support networks.

Because of this I ensure that the content on Balanced Wheel provides a 360-degree view of bereavement support covering the perspectives of someone bereaved or someone providing support, either as a member of their social network or as a professional.

My one wish is that as I continue to journey through my grief that the Balanced Wheel will continue to serve as one of the many agents in bringing our social, faith and work communities closer to being compassionate communities.

Notes

1. https://balancedwheel.co.uk
2. www.cruse.org.uk
3. National Bereavement Alliance (2017) *A Guide to Commissioning Bereavement Services in England*. London: Macmillan Cancer Support.
4. See https://balancedwheel.co.uk/accept-feelings-express-grief-with-words
5. Mayland, C.R., Powell, R.A., Clarke, G.C., Ebenso, B. and Allsop, M.J. (2021) 'Bereavement care for ethnic minority communities: A systematic review of access to, models of, outcomes from, and satisfaction with, service provision.' *PLoS One 16*, 6, e0252188. doi: 10.1371/journal.pone.0252188.

11 Together in Love, Life, and in Death

Maureen Anderson

Maureen is a child of the 1960s, born and raised in Birmingham, England. She says 'I "escaped" this city for the bright lights of London as a naive 19-year-old.' She subsequently chose to go to university as a mature student to study Anthropology, the chosen subject for her enquiring mind, giving her additional licence to be curious about the lives of others:

> I love people and enjoy listening to their stories, observing their quirks, and asking questions for greater understanding. I encourage the people whom I support to journal their own stories, write with their own voices not only because representation matters but because our stories must be told from our experience and not from the perspective of those who oppress us.

Having lost both parents in 2020, she set up 'The Kitchen Table', and describes herself as an adult 'orphan'.[1]

This is not only my story, but it is the story of my family's experience of loss.

In 2020 my parents Sibmora (Syl) and Charles Anderson died. Their death came without fanfare and without any recognition. However, for us, their children, as well as their grandchildren and community, this news came as a complete shock. They died within one month of each other.

In November 2019 we as a family had to make the very hard decision to place our parents in a residential home – a decision that is not considered the 'done thing' in the Black community and, depending on who you speak with, it can feel like you are then judged as wicked, as unloving to your elderly parents, and as selfish. I can hear the comments as I write – 'Ten children and not one of them could look after their parents?'

The truth is that none of us was set up or able to do so because we had not prepared ourselves for this eventuality. We had assumed that our parents would live semi-independently with the wrap-around support from each of us and their carers. Unfortunately, unpredictable health and mobility issues meant that they needed 24-hour care and support. We, their children, and their adult grand-children were all still working or had parental and grandparental responsibilities or jobs abroad, which made it difficult for any one of us to care for them in our own homes, so we did what we thought to be the next best thing.

We chose a local residential home because it was important that family members could continue to visit them daily to carry out their personal care, make sure they had culturally appropriate food, ensure that their hair and skin care regime was maintained and, most importantly for mum and dad, that their spiritual needs were upheld by us and by members of their church. We also made sure that we maintained the continuity of their GP and district nurse team.

During the first phase of the Covid-19 pandemic in 2020 our parents suddenly found themselves isolated. They were confused and alone in the care of the state. They, like so many others, wanted and needed to see their family, and that isolation impacted every-one, including us, their children. Unfortunately, a turn of events happened and the quality of care we expected did not happen.

Dad was rushed to hospital on 26th April 2020 and mum followed 11 days later, which was an extremely stressful time. Dad was overjoyed when he was being discharged into the care of his family, but when we turned up to take him home, he had a fully grown, matted beard, which was odd because he was always clean-shaven. Despite his frailty he was glad to scrub his face and to shave himself with a disposable razor that he could do himself, even though he was bed-ridden.

Mum had not spoken for a few days prior to being admitted to hospital. We do not know the exact date that she stopped talking, but we know that she spoke to my sister on 26th April 2020, which is the day that my sister visited dad after being told that he was at the end of life as he was going into a coma.

We assume that mum must have stopped speaking for about five weeks, and she may also have stopped eating around that same time. We just don't know. We were in horror, shock, upset and disbelief when we saw her, and it turned out that her life expectancy was mere days. To this day we continue to have serious concerns about the care she received.

I was fortunate to spend Father's Day with dad. He and I had always spoken very openly about death, often with humour, but with his faith in mind, so I was able to speak quite candidly to him about it during our last chat together. I reminded him that he had been a good father on earth – firm, with an unfailing love for his family and his faith – and he told me how much he loved all of us and how he felt fortunate that we had all looked after him. That is all that our dad wanted.

During mum's final days she could not speak to us, she could not contribute to moments of reflection or retelling stories, but dad could, so he kept doing his best to ensure that we did not crumble or break by telling us funny, serious and reflective stories. He was giving us the confidence and trust to continue. He engaged with the few visitors and with each child and grandchild. You see, our dad had a lot of faith in the Almighty and an appreciation of each family member's ability to do all that was required to be part of our 'family' team.

We held vigil over our parents, and I was there when mum took her last breath while my siblings were in other rooms, but that last breath went unnoticed. There was no gasp, no gurgling, no tossing or turning, just her quietly slipping away into a deep and everlasting sleep.

Dad, who usually took the lead role in the family, was unable to fully process her passing. He could not bring himself to say any final words out loud, but he did pray for us. When the undertakers came to take mum from the living room where both beds were positioned, he remained in the room with everyone.

After a final goodbye when they placed mum's body in the private ambulance, I slept on the deflated mattress that was mum's bed and my brother slept in the recliner, keeping dad company into the early hours of the next day. Life (as limited as it was) continued for dad for a further four weeks.

I was not there when dad took his last breath, and although I have heard what happened, I find it difficult to imagine his face, his expressions or his sounds. I was not there, and I have found this difficult to reconcile, so I cry and squeeze my eyes tightly shut to stop the tears from falling, and when that doesn't work, sometimes I rather disgustingly use my sleeve to wipe my nose. It can come on so suddenly that I may not have a tissue and I don't want any drips on my laptop.

As a family we didn't have a booklet of what to expect at the end of life and no one asked us if we were aware of the process of dying. In that moment we were just grown-up kids wanting our parents to guide us through this event, as they had done with so many other life events. But this was not to be, as we had no choice but to assume elderhood status and do our best.

So what have I learned? I learned that isolation can be harmful.

That competent healthcare professionals can sometimes make mistakes. That there is a need to provide additional support for families when it comes to providing end of life care, and when conversations about discharge plans are being had with families, the staff should ensure that the information is clearly understood by the family. I also learned that medical teams may not be culturally competent in the way that they deliver end of life care.

As part of my parents' legacy, I now co-host The Kitchen Table, which is a safe space for all to come together once a month to share, listen or celebrate the life of a loved one. I'm glad to be doing something that makes a difference to so many others, and while I still find it extremely upsetting to speak about my family's loss, I know how important it is to share and to release the pain and to be supported.

Taking part in the All-Party Parliamentary Group (APPG) on Hospice and End of Life Care, which is a space where MPs and peers from across the political spectrum campaign for high-quality and accessible palliative and end of life care for all, has helped me somewhat.

As I write this I am still working through the trauma of double loss, and there are times when the closeness of my parents' deaths mean that I don't know which parent I am grieving for. But what I do know is that they are inextricably linked in death, and therefore unsurprisingly in my grieving process they are entwined. My strategy for coping is to take time out of the days that I choose and to be intentional with where I focus my energy and my thoughts. I then focus on one person, and this way I find some comfort in knowing that I have given each of my loved ones their special time.

Poem for Mum

You slipped away yesterday quietly in your sleep
Whilst some were in the kitchen

Some were in their cars
Others in the garden
And children in the park.

You slipped away quietly
Whilst I was in the chair
Having watched you take so many breaths
The last was barely there.

Our mother passed yesterday
A black life that mattered
A black mother who survived many pregnancies
A black woman surviving systems and structures that were against her
A black woman who quietly and confidently raised her children to be
able, confident and deserving adults.

Poem for Dad

Dad you too fell asleep peacefully in your sleep;
I wasn't there this time around to watch or count your breaths,
I wasn't there to monitor your temperature or listen to your chest.
But what I know is we served you, as our father – we were at your
'beck 'n' call' – there's nothing I would do differently despite being
so far away.
I'm glad we had our time together and that you always made me laugh
– like insisting on getting up off the bed forgetting you couldn't
walk!
I'm glad we had our time together – just the two of us – and proud you
were able to pray out loud as we parted on that day.

Rest in Peace Dad – Mum awaits
Your final journey will unite you and you'll really be together always.

Notes

1. www.maureen-anderson.co.uk/what-i-do/the-kitchen-table

12 The Rolling Waves of Black Grief

Jacqueline A. Hinds

Jacqueline is a certified emotional intelligence coach and a leadership consultant. Her expertise lies in building cohesive teams and unlocking the potential of fractured boards, and developing individuals with a strong intellectual, scientific, rational orientation. Jacqueline is passionate about empowering and motivating others, enabling them to be the best that they can be, and has a proven track record of successfully designing bespoke initiatives and delivering a range of services spanning over 20 years as a Human Resources Development specialist, designing and delivering a range of bespoke developmental and coaching initiatives incorporating emotional and intercultural intelligence as a foundation stone in learning.

> *I thought I could swim adequately as the*
> *waves of grief hit me, not once but twice.*
> *The calmness of the water that ebbed and flowed*
> *lulled me into a false sense of security, pulling me under into*
> *a fast flowing current of emotions.*
> *I was lost drowning in my sorrows, battling against the persistent waves*
> *that came crashing down on me, until I realised that*
> *instead of fighting the ongoing flow of emotions, all*
> *I really needed to do was trust the process and*
> *learn to ride the waves of my Black Grief.*

If I knew then what I know now I would've been more prepared to say goodbye! Actually, that is not true! The truth of the matter is, no matter how much time you have to prepare for a loved one's departure from this mortal realm, it will never be enough to prepare you for their eventual day of departure.

My story of grief and loss came in two waves. Wave One: my mother's passing in 2009, and Wave Two: my father's passing 16 months to the day from my mother in 2010. Two different experiences of grief and loss, two different stories, connected by a silk thread that runs through family, entrenched in heritage, love and respect.

Wave One

Blossom was my mother's name, and when she introduced herself to people, she always said she was the prettiest flower in her mother and father's garden, hence her name. She came to England at the tender age of 16, with two younger siblings, to join her parents who came over with other Black people from the Caribbean islands during the Windrush period.

My mother lived in Jamaica having 'gone back home' for good in 1997 after going backwards and forwards while she was building her house there – a normal practice for many Black people back then. They would spend six months 'back home' and then six months in England, sorting out their medical requirements, appointments and other things.

I was always calling my mum and having long conversations with her, especially when she was in Jamaica. I remember calling her during Hurricane Gilbert, which hit Jamaica in 1988. She had just finished building her house and I could hear the storm raging around it, which was very frightening from my end as I'd never experienced this type of storm before. Although I wasn't there, just hearing the sound of the storm through the phone evoked enough pictures in my mind for me to feel frightened. Thank goodness there was minimal damage to the house, so I was thankful that all the hard work and money my mother had spent in building her house had not been impacted by the storm's raging swell.

My mother was very special to me, and one of the most significant times in my life was when she came over in 2007 to spend time with her tenth grandson. I had given birth to my son at the age of 44, at the same time as I was working as a consultant at Imperial College Healthcare NHS Trust, supporting them through their transformational change in merging two healthcare organisations and an educational institute. I considered it too good an opportunity to let pass by, so my mother came over to support me while spending time with her new grandson who was three months old. It was not only timely, but also a precious moment in the timeline leading up to her leaving us.

Nothing seemed different with my mum's health when I saw her, but when she came back the following year to visit and attend my son's dedication (christening), I noticed that she was a lot slimmer and looked very tired. When I commented on how much weight she had lost, my mum brushed off my comment and concerns, putting it down to working hard doing the cooking and feeding the workers she employed to tend her sugarcane field. I was very wary and concerned, and so too were my siblings.

It was then that my older brother decided to take her to BE-DOC Health Care Services. As soon as they saw my mother, they informed us that they needed to give her a full health check-up. They, too, were concerned, and after conducting a series of tests they gave us information that we weren't prepared for – mum had stage 4 stomach cancer.

My siblings and I were shocked to the core and never expected to hear this diagnosis. First, the doctors had to stabilise her diabetes as it was out of control, and then give her a blood transfusion and blood pressure tablets. Then they gave her the option of surgery to excise the mass in her stomach with the latest state-of-the-art laser surgery technology, but my mother refused the treatment. She just did not want to undergo any form of surgery, and was adamant about that no matter how we encouraged her to do so.

I remember having a conversation with my mother before she decided to go back to Jamaica. She said, 'Jacqueline, I just don't want to be cut any more!' My mother had had a traumatic experience after giving birth to my youngest brother and that had put her off any form of operation – no matter how lifesaving. I remember that I was bathing my young son as she spoke, and I started to cry. Although I was heartbroken at her decision not to have the operation, I totally understood where she was coming from – but understanding didn't lessen the fact that my mother was going to die.

In early 2009 my mother requested that all her children visit her where she was staying in the USA after having spent some time at Uchee Pines Institute, Alabama – a place of respite, nutrition and faith. Her cancer was too far gone, and she said that she just needed her children around her, like 'olive branches'.

We all made the journey, and in the midst of our varying levels of grief, this was a divinely surreal experience for everyone. Just as Abraham in the Bible blessed each of his sons, so my mother blessed each of her children and their families, and it is an experience that I will carry with me until the day my time comes to depart from this mortal realm. I can't explain the range of emotions I went through, but as a woman of Faith I knew the Almighty was guiding, supporting and comforting us along our journey and preparation of saying goodbye to our mother.

My mother, mentor and best friend passed away on 30th July 2009. The night of my mother's passing I slept like a baby, knowing she was finally at peace, asleep and no longer in pain.

When it came to fulfilling my mother's final wishes, we decided to hold a celebration of life service for her in our hometown of

Bedford, where we had all grown up, with her internment on her property in Jamaica.

The final journey

After mum's memorial service my two younger siblings and I flew to Jamaica a week ahead of the rest of the family to prepare everything ahead of her funeral. On the day of departure, we set off to the airport and arrived really early. We checked our luggage in and stopped for a hot drink on the way to the departure gate. After finishing our drinks, we made our way to the departure gate only to be informed that the doors to the aeroplane had already been closed and that we would be missing this flight.

I felt as though we had been treading in treacle. I couldn't understand how time had elapsed so quickly; it almost seemed as if we had slowed down and the world around us was running at the normal pace and time. In the depths of my grief, I felt calm. The staff were empathetic and were able to get us on another flight but this time stopping at Boston, USA, and from there we would catch a connecting flight at 5:00 am the next morning, bound for Jamaica.

The saying 'everything happens for a reason' was very pertinent because what was in store for us in Jamaica when we landed was a whole new chapter of emotions and grief. When we finally laid our mother to rest, we knew that it was our faith that had kept us going through all the trials and tribulations we faced.

Arriving back in England we settled down to life without mum. It was hard. There were times when I would pick up the phone, ready to dial her number in Jamaica. After a moment I'd realise that she wouldn't be there to pick up the phone and have a conversation. Before her passing I would sometimes ring her two or three times just to have a chat and, I remember one day her saying to me on the second or third time I'd rung her, 'Jacqueline, what the rice and peas you want?' She always made me laugh and gave me solid words of wisdom. I miss those precious times with her.

Although she has gone, the memories and good times will always live on in my heart.

Wave Two

Our second wave of grief came just 16 months to the day of my mother's passing.

My parents divorced when I was in my teens, and we didn't have much contact with our father, and in 1994 I lost contact with him completely. Then one day my youngest brother called to say that my father was battling bladder cancer and had had an operation that had changed the quality of his life, and even though I had a young daughter at the time, I did my best to rally round and support him.

In the years that followed, my siblings and I re-established our relationship with our father, and when my mum would come over to England she would go and 'look for him'. That was quite nice to see because I think my father never stopped caring for our mum, and they had an amicable relationship.

To be honest, when I look back on the timeline of events, I think my father's health started to decline not long after my mum was diagnosed with cancer in 2007. When he found out that she had been diagnosed with cancer, he became very quiet, and over the course of a few weeks there seemed to be quite a few incidents happening. He began to complain of dizziness and chronic back pain, which the doctors were unable to get to the bottom of.

In late 2009, after my mother's passing, we got a call to inform us that our father had been hospitalised. We all quickly rushed over there to find out that he'd had one of his dizzy spells, fallen over and hit his head against the radiator and had been lying undiscovered for 12 hours. The trauma of that dreadful experience really impacted his health so much that he was unable to walk and refused to engage in any rehabilitation sessions. He got angry.

One day, when my sister and I went to visit him in the reha-bilitation unit, he was at an all-time low and feeling very sorry for himself. He was so fed up with not being able to do the things that he wanted to do because of his immobility that he blurted out that he wished he could just end it all.

You can imagine how shocked we were to hear him say that. My mum used to say, 'you have to take bad things and laugh', so even though what he said was no laughing matter, we reminded him that it was nigh on impossible for him to end it as he was immobile and not even trying to walk. The thought that his immobility meant he couldn't even carry out his threat must have really scared him because on our next visit we were pleasantly surprised that he was up and walking around the unit.

After his discharge a few weeks later, as a family we continued to care for our father with my older brother being his main carer, administering medication and accompanying him to appointments. But my dad continued to complain of constant back pain, so we kept pleading with the doctor to refer him for a body scan. We later found out that additional tests had been carried out but the results weren't shared with us.

It was during that time that I started a course on Black Lead-ership in White Organisations at the Tavistock NHS Trust Uni-versity – a controversial but very much-needed course – and it helped me to understand the inequalities of healthcare, leadership and progression, and the systemic racism in healthcare that Black people have been facing for a long time. I can't help wondering if this systemic problem contributed to the care my father received.

Time was passing by, yet the painkillers were not actually do-ing anything to ease the pain our father was suffering. Although we grew up going to church our father never went to church or adhered to any practices or principles of any church body – but I do distinctly remember the day he gave his heart to God. It was

30th October 2010. The date is also my birthday, so I was delighted when he repented his sins and took the stance to commit to being a Christian.

But the gladness turned to sadness in exactly four weeks. I was in my final session with my course supervisor when halfway through I noticed my phone was silently vibrating. I picked it up, cancelled the call and put it back in my bag, but it started vibrating again. I once again cancelled the call. It was only when it started vibrating again that my supervisor told me to take the call as it was probably urgent. I wasn't prepared for what I heard. It was my younger sister calling me to let me know that our father had passed away in his sleep.

I was totally caught off guard. The shock was overwhelming. The date of our father's passing was 30th November 2010, which is 16 months to the day that our mother had passed on 30th July 2009.

In our grief we mobilised as a Black family to give our father a wonderful send-off, trying our best not to treat anyone, including the extended family, unfairly, or to inadvertently ignore or forget to call someone. That was a challenge because we have a large family on our father's side, but we did our best to avoid adding another layer to the grieving process to an already grieving family.

Grief is part of this journey we call life, and I embrace it and work with it because I cannot stop the waves of grief from coming.

13 Death, Grief, Loss and Bereavement During Covid-19

Natalie Darko

Natalie is associate professor at the University of Leicester and director of Inclusion at the Leicester NIHR Biomedical Research Centre. Natalie specialises in health research and practice that addresses equality, equity and the inclusion of underrepresented and minority groups. She has extensive experience in leading and delivering research within the field of health inequalities, of which her current research projects focus on maternal health, womb cancer, social prescribing, diabetes, faith-based interventions and dementia. She supports researchers, organisations and practitioners, nationally and internationally, on how to work collaboratively with underrepresented groups, to inform equitable health and research practice.

There have been an unprecedented number of deaths, with nearly 6 million people dying globally from Covid-19.[1]

Unfortunately, Covid-19 has not impacted all population groups equally. Across the globe, racially minoritised groups have been hardest hit by the pandemic. Research examining minority ethnic groups in the UK has shown striking racial and ethnic inequalities in Covid-19 mortality.[2] A disproportionate number of Covid-19 deaths have occurred among Black African and African Caribbean groups – groups that have subsequently been exposed to insurmountable levels of loss and profound grief.

This chapter will provide an understanding of racial and ethnic differences in the experiences of death, loss and grieving. It will explore personal and lived experiences of grief, loss and bereavement and the impact of death on mental wellbeing for Black African and African Caribbean groups during the Covid-19 pandemic It will also provide recommendations for supporting Black African and African Caribbean people who have experienced the death of a loved one.

Racial and ethnic differences

Between 2020 and 2021, people from Black African, Black African Caribbean and Black British groups experienced a higher risk of Covid-19 mortality than White groups, even after adjusting for age, demographic and socio-economic factors and pre-existing health conditions.[3]

There are multiple reasons for this, including the systemic racism and inequalities that exist in healthcare, housing and employment.[4] Another is the existence of health conditions such as obesity, type 2 diabetes and high blood pressure. The prevalence of such conditions among Black African and Black African Caribbean groups is arguably the result of long-standing racial inequalities and systemic racism.[5]

Although death rates are now slowing, we cannot forget the multitude of losses Black African and African Caribbean groups have had to overcome as a result of their experiences of inequality during the pandemic. Society needs to learn from these experiences, as grief and loss remain, and there will be other pandemics in the future.

Loss and grieving

During the height of the Covid-19 pandemic, millions of people experienced loss, grief and bereavement due to the death of family, friends and loved ones. Below I will explore what these terms really mean.

'Bereavement' is experienced following a loss, and is often used interchangeably with 'grief', yet they have different meanings. 'Bereavement' refers to the process of adjusting to a loss. 'Grief' is the multifaceted reaction to a loss or death.[6] Following a bereavement, individuals experience grief in different ways – it may be 'normal' and uncomplicated, or complicated and prolonged, moving through various stages of grief.[7]

'Loss' has a wider focus, and is often defined as being deprived of a person or a possession. Beyond the personal loss caused by death, loss impacts other areas of people's lives, and so grief is also experienced in the loss of people's hope, future, employment, interaction and partnerships. These are 'symbolic losses' that could stem from the primary loss, and that can have a devastating impact on the grief experienced.

During the pandemic, experiences of loss and grief were also compounded by the restrictions placed on losing someone at the end of life. Specifically, death was experienced through windows in intensive care units, over phone calls and via screens. The pandemic has impacted on people's ability to conduct spiritual and religious practices, and the impact of this appears to have been greater in Black minority populations compared to White groups.[8]

Body disposal and social distancing guidelines imposed during the pandemic have not allowed for spiritual and cultural processes of mourning to be practised within Black African and African Caribbean communities. The loss of spiritual, traditional and cultural practices that assist in the grieving process for these populations has impacted significantly on the collective experiences of these communities – for example, long-standing traditions among certain Jamaican Christian funeral customs, such as the practice of the Nine Night celebrations, also known as the 'dead yard'[9] during which relatives and friends gather over nine consecutive evenings to celebrate the life of the deceased until a final night of celebration.

Such challenges have made grieving more complicated for many who are accustomed to spiritual and religious practices. And given the higher rates of Covid-19 mortality among Black African and African Caribbean minorities, the impact of experiences has been even more profound. Despite this, limited attention was given to understanding how Black African and African Caribbean groups coped with death, grief, loss and bereavement during the pandemic in the UK.

To address this, the voices of the groups who have experienced death and loss during the pandemic are presented here. The people who have shared their experiences in this chapter did so as part of one-hour research interviews completed by the researcher (a Black mixed-race female) during the 2021 pandemic and national lockdowns in the UK. Participants were asked to comment on their experiences of death and loss during the pandemic, and the impact of the control measures on their health. The interview data provided was analysed for common themes.

In accordance with the ethical approvals awarded to the research, the identities of the participants have been anonymised. The participants were males (10) and females (20), between the ages of 25 and 75. They self-identified as British Black African, Black African Caribbean and Black Mixed, born in the UK or migrated to the UK from Africa or the Caribbean at a younger age. They were all currently or previously employed in the public sector.

Personal and lived experiences

All the participants discussed experiences of losing relatives, friends and loved ones due to Covid-19. In their discussions about death, the majority felt that systematic inequalities embedded in employment were fundamental drivers of these outcomes. Several of the participants explained that their loved ones and friends were located in high-risk, low-income and insecure employment, and this had contributed to their death.

For example, two Black African Caribbean women explained that they had lost close (Caribbean) relatives who had been employed in insecure contracts, with limited access to sick leave. Their relatives were subsequently required to return to work before they had recovered from the virus for fear of being unable to financially support their families. Unfortunately, both relatives later died from Covid-19. For these women their experience of loss and subsequent grief was more traumatic than other White groups, because they felt there had been an injustice in death – their loved ones had experienced death because of the inequalities they experienced in access to secure employment.

One African Caribbean women (civil servant, 35) explains:

Black people like us...are always suffering, we have been struggling and making do for years, but now with Covid it's added to the suffering, we don't have access to the same pay as others and so when we get sick, we are supposed to just carry on and keep up the good dutiful work. But we are losing everyone and it's unjust!... We lost our mum, because she had to keep working to support the rest of the family, but it cost her, her life and now she's gone.

Similarly, one African Caribbean woman (healthcare professional, 55) explained:

Covid has shown us what we've been dealing with for years... rubbish jobs and less money. We lost dad, he'd been in the same job for years, doing it for as long as he could, to look after us all. But it was like he was in an ongoing slot machine – he was unable to take time off when he got sick, so he just kept going... but nobody [at work] listened...eventually it took him.

For those participants who were employed in high-risk key worker roles, the experience of witnessing death and the risk of death from Covid-19 was emotionally difficult. The grief they experienced in watching so many people from all ethnic backgrounds dying was emotionally troublesome in their jobs, but witnessing higher numbers of people from their own racial and ethnic background dying and suffering at the end of their lives was even more problematic for them. For example, one African male participant (clinician, 50) explained:

Honestly, most days it's just too much for me...particularly at the start of the pandemic...so many of our patients were dying and they are just like me. But there isn't anything to support us, we are all just dying and does anyone really care...what will be done to support us? I worry everyday about dying. I'm trying to save our lives...but I'm worried I won't make it out.

Unfortunately, for the majority of the participants, structural inequalities embedded in employment disadvantaged them, which had the most damaging effect on their experiences of death, grief and loss during the pandemic.

The impact of death on mental wellbeing

'Be resilient and grieve silently'

A core theme that arose from the participants' discussion of their experiences of death was resilience, and the importance of being emotionally resilient. What is interesting about the participants' discussion of being resilient in coping with death is that they had become accustomed to death. With so many members of their communities dying, many felt that they had to be emotionally resilient to manage the losses. As we saw in the comments made above, those who had died or were working with patients dying from Covid-19 felt they needed to manage the ongoing grief and keep going.

Many of the interviewees who had migrated to the UK from the Caribbean presented similar narratives of being emotionally resilient in how they managed the loss of family and friends. However, they also felt that their ability to cope was in part due to the endless loss and grief they had already experienced in their lives as Caribbean diaspora. For those who had migrated at a young age to the UK, their journeys were often described as periods of prolonged grief, due to the loss of connections with loved ones, friends and family back in the Caribbean, but also for the loss of those they had to leave behind. One male African Caribbean participant (key worker, 63) explained:

> Our move from the Caribbean as children and losing of family back home has been hard enough. But now with Covid it's just more loss, the constant death of family members who have suffered from poor health from being here and now it's us! But...we just keep it getting up...pushing forward...we have to be strong and just deal with it because we don't have a choice... who's going to listen.

Similarly, one of the African Caribbean female participants (retired civil servant, 75) discussed the loss of a family member dying from Covid-19 and the ongoing grief that had resulted from her migration to the UK. Her discussion centres on being emotionally resilient in her management of grief:

We are a generation who has had to recover from a lot of the unseen trauma that we had when we were moved from the Caribbean as kids...the loss of relationships with our parents (left behind) and we've had to adapt into the different kind of situations we all find ourselves in. I lost my mum, she died when she was in her 20s back home, it was sudden. Now we are still losing more family in Covid. So, I really feel that we've dealt with so much loss and it is unseen, it's never talked about [by the government] or dealt with either. You know we'll most probably die and still be not heard...but you stay strong because you have to.

'No one's listening and supporting us!'

What's apparent in these comments and so many of the other interviews is that many feel that no one is listening to them or supporting them in dealing with the endless death, grief and loss.

For all the participants, they felt that those who claimed to listen didn't seem to understand them, and the provision of culturally appropriate interventions and coping mechanisms for people from the African diaspora were significantly limited. Furthermore, there seemed to be minimal equality in representation and a commitment to the principle of practice that grief services were delivered with them and involved them. One of the participants explained how she had responded to this and was addressing what she felt was institutional racism:

As far as I'm concerned, there is still institutional racism...particularly in health and care provision. I needed to do something myself to help people like us, so I provide support to Black communities who are suffering and who just not supported by health services. We are assumed to be strong...just because we are Black...but where is the support for us. We are supporting and caring for our own because the services don't cater for us! I've had to go and mediate for Black patients and families dealing with cancer and death because they're not being listened to. With Covid and all this death in our communities, you'd think things would have changed but it hasn't.

Many of the participants also felt that restrictions on spiritual, religious and traditional practices and access to Black-led organisations had impacted negatively on the support provided for them dealing with grief and bereavement. The inability to attend these organisations and the associated collective support networks led to feelings of social isolation and low mental wellbeing. This was impacted further by the loss of financial support during Covid-19 for organisations supporting Black communities. For example, one male African Caribbean participant (religious leader, 65) explained:

What people forget is that for many people, Christian faith is a collective faith. We provide support for people to come together and support each other in times of loss. The restrictions have meant many people couldn't come to pray or be with others, but now because so many of our communities are dying from this virus, people don't want to come to church. Most already have underlying health conditions so the fear of Covid, of dying and even being blamed for spreading Covid means people are still staying away to stay safe. But the problem we have is that people are housebound and dealing with losing their relatives all alone. We can't get out to help them or host community events because we now can't afford to maintain our buildings. We couldn't even afford the internet...so our people are alone and suffering more than before.

Recommendations for supporting Black African and African Caribbean people

It is evident that much more support is needed to help Black African and Black African Caribbean people to cope with death, loss, grief and bereavement during and following the Covid-19 pandemic and beyond. Disparities in the Covid-19 mortality rates have highlighted that Black African and African Caribbean groups experienced much higher levels of loss and grief than other White groups.

Despite this, the personal narratives presented here show that these minority groups felt 'unheard' and 'unseen' in their experiences of grief, loss and bereavement during the pandemic. Subsequently, much further recognition needs to be given to these feelings of not being listened to by practitioners, service providers, commissioners and policy makers.

More attention should also be given to the multiple and ongoing losses specific groups experienced during the pandemic, but also in their migration histories and the structural inequalities that ultimately lead to more complicated and prolonged experiences of grief.

Strategies for coping with loss are embedded in collective practices and traditions, and delivered by Black-led community organisations, faith centres, churches and Black African and Black African Caribbean people themselves. The belief in emotional resilience and 'carrying on' in times of loss should be acknowledged further, but not as a reason to perceive these groups as hard to reach or difficult to engage in discussing their grief. Rather, practitioners should recognise its existence and for some, the important role it plays in caring for their own families, friends and communities.

It is evident that the people interviewed were not unwilling to talk about their experiences of death, loss and grief. However, it is important to be reflective about the positioning of the researcher – my identity as a Black mixed-race woman. Did my positioning impact on why the interviewees were comfortable sharing these concerns with me? Was there an assumption made by the participants that my racial identity allowed me to have a shared understanding of the personal experiences of death and its impact on Black communities? This cannot be known without further questioning.

Either way, other practitioners and service providers who do not share racial and ethnic identities with Black African and Black African Caribbean people need to work to build trust and recognise their feelings of being unsupported, not listened to and blamed for the health inequalities they face.

Commissioners and policy makers need to do much more to engage with, support and fund Black-led and faith organisations, as well as the community support networks they help to create. Given the ongoing and prolonged levels of grief experienced, support cannot be short term: ongoing provision and long-term trust should be our goal.

And finally, and importantly, this should not be an engagement that is about Black populations without their involvement!

Notes

1. WHO (World Health Organization) (2022) 'WHO Coronavirus (COVID-19) Dashboard.' https://covid19.who.int

2. White, C. and Nafilyan, V. (2020) 'Coronavirus (COVID-19) related deaths by ethnic group, England and Wales: 2 March 2020 to 15 May 2020.' Newport: Office for National Statistics.

3. ONS (Office of National Statistics) (2022) 'Updating ethnic contrasts in deaths involving the coronavirus (COVID-19), England: 8 December 2020 to 1 December 2021.' Newport: ONS.

4. www.manchester.ac.uk/discover/news/extent-of-uks-race-inequality/

5. Chouhan, K. and Nazroo, L. (2020) 'Health Inequalities.' In B. Byrne, C. Alexander, O. Khan, J. Nazroo and W. Shankley (eds) *Ethnicity, Race and Inequality in the UK: State of the Nation* (pp.73–92). Bristol: Policy Press; Nazroo, J. (2003) 'The structuring of ethnic inequalities in health: Economic position, racial discrimination, and racism.' *American Journal of Public Health 93*, 2, 277–284. doi: 10.2105/ajph.93.2.277.

6. Bruce, C.A. (2007) 'Helping patients, families, caregivers, and physicians, in the grieving process.' Journal of Osteopathic Medicine *107*, 7, E33–E40; Buglass, E. (2010) 'Grief and

bereavement theories.' Nursing Standard 24, 41, 44–47. doi: 10.7748/ns2010.06.24.41.44. c7834.

7. Zisook, S. and Shear, K. (2009) 'Grief and bereavement: What psychiatrists need to know.' *World Psychiatry: Official Journal of the World Psychiatric Association (WPA) 8*, 2, 67–74. doi: 10.1002/j.2051-5545.2009.tb00217.x.

8. Routen, A., Darko, N., Willis, A., Miksza, J. and Khunti, K. (2021) '"It's so tough for us now" – COVID-19 has negatively impacted religious practices relating to death among minority ethnic groups.' *Public Health 194*, 146–148. doi: 10.1016/j.puhe.2021.03.007.

9. Petgrave-Nelson, L. (2021) 'COVID-19 reflection: From the diary of a Black social worker.' *Journal of Social Work in End-of-Life & Palliative Care 17*, 2–3, 120–123. https://doi.org/10 .1080/15524256.2021.1915921

14 Miscarriage, Stillbirth and Infant Loss

Karen Carberry

Karen is a family and systemic psychotherapist, former executive director, trustee and acting chair of the Association for Family Therapy (AFT);[1] advisory board member of Humanity Summit; head of Family and Systemic Therapy for Orri, a specialist eating disorders clinic;[2] and supervisor for HOPE Bereavement Support,[3] an organisation specialising in infant and child loss, bereavement and trauma. Karen is also a visiting lecturer at the University of Oxford Doctorate in Clinical Psychology Programme, and is a new grandmother. Her current research interest is the national Culturally-Adapted Family Intervention Study (Ca-FI), led by Professor Dawn Edge, where Karen is co-lead supervisor with Professor Katherine Berry at the University of Manchester. Karen is co-editor of The International Handbook of Black Community Mental Health *(Emerald Publishing, 2020) and* Therapy In Colour: Anti-Racist and Intercultural Approaches by Therapists of Colour *(Jessica Kingsley Publishers, 2023).*

The impact of miscarriage, stillbirth and infant loss on women and their families is far reaching across generations, and can often be a taboo subject in Black, Brown and Asian communities. The physical effects of loss and grief are further compounded by challenges in mental health, juxtaposed by the alarming disparity in the outcomes in pregnancy for Black and Asian women and their babies compared to White women. Understanding the lived experiences and cultural interventions to appropriately enhance dignity and care through the pregnancy pathway is key, together with access to culturally appropriate training for medical teams and therapists delivering counselling services and support groups, to help clients and their families process the loss of their loved ones and begin to heal.

Introduction

The history of childbirth and midwifery, for Black and Asian women, has been tumultuous. For those unfamiliar with the term 'obstetrics', it is defined as the field of medicine associated with childbirth and midwifery.[4] Black women were enslaved for centuries as breeding stock for profit[5] and as medical subjects for the performing of experimental procedures by renowned physicians such as Dr James Marion Sims, cited as the 'father of gynaecology'. Without consent, and for four years, Dr Sims experimented on 40 Black women, without anaesthesia. He then went on to offer and provide the same procedure to wealthy White women, but this time administered with anaesthesia.[6] This lack of regard to the Black woman's body has been well documented and has increased the tension between the disparity of care between White, Asian and Black mothers in pregnancy.

Black women are misunderstood when it comes to their responses to distress in birth and perinatal experiences.[7] The links to depression and their need for counselling goes unheard[8], and instead they are offered psychotropic treatment such as antidepressants.[9] Notions of Black and Brown women having a higher pain threshold than White women are often symbolic of the 'strong Black women trope', possibly inadvertently internalised, and applied by what nurses and midwives may have been taught in training and systematically applied in practice.[10] The lack of adherence to diagnosis and treatment for the manifestation of extreme pain in the field of obstetrics, and its notable history of littered tragedies regarding the loss of mothers in childbirth and the death of a child or both through literature, on-screen adaptations and news media, remains a huge concern for Black people and people of colour. In many cultures the death of a child appears to be so tangible – there is a death, a death certificate and a burial. These events mark the life of a child much loved, and unforgotten. What of the children who have not quite made it out of the womb alive, or just after birth? Who is allowed to call these children babies, and provide the space to grieve the loss of a vision of life? Or, in the case of the family, looking for medical support while managing the distress of the expectant mother, who is then robbed of life and may have also has passed away alongside her baby? The recent publications of reports on the demise of women in childbirth and/or their babies has struck a chord of disbelief, fear, anger and anguish in many Black and Brown families who have been devastated by grief.[11]

As a family and systemic psychotherapist for over 25 years, I have seen, without doubt, that when there is a death in the family, everyone is affected. Yet for women who lose children through miscarriage, stillbirth and infant loss, there appears to be a bit of a hierarchy in allowable expressions of loss in miscarriage.[12] This bias extends to the loss of Black and Asian women in childbirth, the disparity in infant mortality and maternal deaths, which demands a process of action and outward mourning.

Black people and people of colour, who have had a healthy cultural suspicion to medicine and therapy, are worried about being looked after appropriately by the medical profession.[13] Black mothers and women of colour, and their partners, as a result of adverse experiences in childbirth, hold a position of hope in raising their existing and surviving children, while simultaneously experiencing high levels of anxiety, often turned into advocacy regarding the survival for both mothers and babies prevailing statistics of mothers dying in pregnancy[14] and high rates of infant mortality (MBRRACE-UK 2020), as described in Figure 1.

FIGHTING TO SURVIVE: DECOLONISING MATERNAL EXPERIENCES 2020/21

Birth Experiences of Black Women
- Black women in the UK are 4 times more likely than white women to die in pregnancy or childbirth. (MBBRACE, 2020)
- 40 per 100,000 pregnancies

Birth Experiences of Black Infants
- Stillbirth rates for Black and Black British babies were over twice those for white babies, whilst neonatal death rates were 45% higher.
- For babies of Asian and Asian British ethnicity, stillbirth and neonatal death rates were both around 60% higher than for babies of white ethnicity.
- The stillbirth rate was 1 in 295 for white babies; 1 in 188 for Asian babies and 1 in 136 for Black babies. (MBBRACE, 2020)

© Karen Carberry 17/05/2021

Figure 1: Fighting to survive – decolonising maternal experiences, 2020–21

Figure 1 highlights deaths included in reported mortality rates, which you can see is highly concerning. Year on year there is a much higher prevalence of Black women from all socio-economic backgrounds, at risk of dying in pregnancy or childbirth compared to White mothers. In addition, in the UK, black babies are twice as likely to encounter stillbirth, and Black neonatal deaths are 45 per cent more likely than White neonatal deaths (MBRRACE, 2020).

Cultural considerations

The process many women go through to achieve their vision of motherhood can take many attempts and turns. However, in my work with women and men in their journey to create a family, I have often found their relentlessness and courage to succeed deeply moving. I have also found that because of their experiences, some women go on to make a difference in the processes and policies to achieve an equitable cultural responsiveness from professionals.

In the following case vignette,[15] I had the privilege to speak with Ms. Ansa Ahmed, CEO of HOPE Bereavement Support, who courageously shared some of her personal story of miscarriage and infant loss, which then became the driving force for setting up her charity. The reader should take caution in reading further, and should approach organisations for support if they feel overwhelmed by the text.

Vignette: The importance of care

Ansa: So...my journey started over 15 years ago, I felt I was not able to talk to anyone in my community and contacted miscarriage associations including SANDS.

Karen: It was taboo...because of what?

Ansa: Taboo subject because it is to be with reproduction. From a South Asian perspective, it would be lewd to talk about anything to do with my body, or reproduction, or anything to do with sexual acts. You can't talk to anyone. I had support from my family, in that they were able to say 'I am sorry for your loss'.

Ansa then gave some information about some of her losses during previous pregnancies.

At 5 weeks: Molar loss. When there is a problem with a fertilised egg which means a baby and a placenta do not develop the way they should during pregnancy, a molar pregnancy will not be able to survive.[16] It happens by chance and is rare.

At 11–12 weeks loss: Yoke sap collapse. This is the collapse of the structure that provides the embryo with nourishment.

At 19–20 weeks loss: I was in labour for five days.

At 20 weeks loss: Literally my baby was born and lived for 45 minutes, breathed, and then died in front of my eyes.

While I was in labour, they [professionals] were getting me to sign papers that said that I understand that they will not be doing anything without my consent, and that I will not sue them.

Karen: Did you receive any counselling?

Ansa: You can't talk about mental health in our community... because translated it is 'crazy'. However, I started to become more active and speak out, and I wanted to make it better for the women's experience. I got involved with a research project with Leeds University. They did some research to see why the infant deaths in South Asian and Caribbean children were so high. It was a space to get a few women together and it was a...space.

In 2012 I started to go to a friend of mine, a breastfeeding buddy group, and we talked about all the adversities we had experienced, and she said, 'Why don't you do something about it, there should be something done about it', and we both then set up support groups. A colleague in the Black Health Initiative [community engagement organisation working towards equality of access to education, health and social care in Leeds] was the first person who supported me. I was then able to train as a counsellor through Child Bereavement UK. After we trained, we were able to set up support groups. Lived experience is one thing, but I wanted to make sure that I got it right. We had a couple of other colleagues who were part of Haamla, and we brought in primary care, who had Doulas and interpreters. [Haamla Service is part of the Leeds Teaching Hospitals NHS Trust and provides advocacy in the midwifery service, bilingual maternity support workers and antenatal groups with an additional option of translators].

Karen: Very inspiring! Can you tell me why you set up the Rainbow Mamas Support group?

Ansa: Child loss is so isolating, it feels very unjust, and one gets lost in an abyss when that dream shatters, and nine times out of ten you cannot get closure because the doctors cannot find the reason why this keeps happening. A majority of people who suffer miscarriage are Black and Asian.

Karen: What are the similarities and differences you have observed across cultures?

Ansa: White women were saying that they were being avoided by friends, and the Black and Asian women were made to feel that they should 'pick yourself up and get on with it'. There was a lot of self-shame about their bodies, and blame, and you did not see that in the White women. In the Black women there has been thousands of years of fighting against adversity [but there is shame in talking about it]. [Ansa uses an Arabic word] In Arabic the term is translated as 'have some shame...don't talk about these things'.

When I was pregnant I wanted to hold my belly and yet I was told 'Why are you pushing your belly out'... Now I am thinking about the media...when we saw, Meghan, the Duchess of Sussex, and she was holding her tummy, the media criticised her, and when her sister-in-law Catherine, the Duchess of Cambridge, now Princess of Wales, showed her she belly, the media said 'how beautiful and blossoming'.

Karen: Is there something about not being able to own the womanly part of you? And then the other thing I frequently hear about, is the experiences of when Black women go into the hospital... I am holding my tummy as I speak about this.

Ansa: I am holding mine. [*We both have an embodied response to this conversation*]

Ansa: When I lost my first [baby] Tariq, I had excellent support... and went into psychosis...so the year before, I was told you cannot conceive naturally...and when I went to IVF, I was told I was too fat... Fat shamed...rather than told voluptuous... And I went into agoraphobia. I could not go out for six months. I was completely shattered. I was a successful woman, had my own house, and car and career, and I was shattered.

Karen: [*Reflecting internally, I think there is something about the way the bodies of women of colour are pitted against White woman, specifically in regard to Body Mass Index (BMI)*] It is a travesty, that Black women's natural shape is stigmatised in the West, and this seems to be expanding across the globe. I am quite passionate about how this is intending to impact the mental wellbeing of Black women and all women of colour. However, there is currently a body positivity movement taking place in resistance. [*I notice that Ansa has paused; I ask her if she would like to stop or continue; she motions that she wants to continue*]

Ansa: ...and then I was pregnant, and it was a miracle child, and 20 weeks later I had my signed papers to force an induced labour because I had gone into psychosis... I went home and got my teddy and put my dead baby's clothes onto my teddy... I suddenly came to myself...and threw the teddy away and fell on my knees, and cried out to Allah...and at this point the door bell rang, it was midwives – and they said 'Hi Mrs Ahmed, we came to weigh your beautiful baby boy'...but they got to the wrong house, and I said to them, you will come back to my door and you will weigh my son.

Five years later the student midwife who stood behind them came and recognised me and my son Mustafa and came to weigh my daughter. She [the midwife] was crying...as she remembered my journey.

Karen: This is so moving, supernatural even, this witnessing of your prophecy five years earlier. I am so pleased for you. In what way has this witnessing taken you further on your journey to impact the medical profession and help other families?

Ansa: I was asked to go to Leeds University to talk to their predominately White doctors and midwives...to speak about my good and bad experience and teach them how to speak to Black and Brown mothers.

Karen: How was this received?

Ansa: I went in with a hijab [meaning 'partition' or 'curtain', a scarf that covers the head]...and then with a suit underneath my clothes...and then they would just ignore me...and then when I took it off, I asked them 'Do they feel better now?'

During their medical training I talked about my three near-death experiences and the lack of continuity of care. I suggested improvements, including asking the mother whether she wants to bathe the child [after the baby has died], and the opportunity to be given the afterbirth for burial; and providing different stairs/lifts to leave the building when a mother has just experience child loss. Having her go down into a lift with a mother who has given birth and is taking her live baby home when another has lost their baby to death is uncaring. There should be clear guidance if you cannot afford the burial, and inform mothers/parents of their rights, specifically if they are affected by the immigration process. There should also be information on the sudden onset of psychosis after loss or multiple losses, and include support when one can gets stuck in the grieving process.

Karen: Thank you, Ansa, for sharing parts of your journey; it is very powerful and moving, and I feel honoured to be able to share some of your story. I can certainly see the impetus for starting this organisation to help all parties associated with the grief and loss, together with support groups to help mothers and their families to move forward with hope for strengthened mental health wellbeing. Thank you.

After the interview I checked in with Ansa to see how she was doing, and that she had enough support after sharing her story. Ansa, who is also a counsellor, had put into place some time for self-care. Although we have not shared all details of all her children who have passed on, they are not forgotten, as it is important that they should, and must, be acknowledged.[17]

Counselling and the psychotherapy process of working with women of colour who are pregnant and experienced loss

If you are looking to access interventions by working with a counsellor, or are in the therapy field, developing coping strategies alongside some counselling support is a recommended process.

However, due to austerity, counselling tends to be offered on a short-term basis. I use the terms 'counselling' and 'psychotherapy', 'counsellor' and 'therapist' interchangeably here to denote the clinician providing therapeutic support to clients. These could range between 3 and 12 sessions if accessed via the GP, NHS, through an employee's Employment Assistance Programme (EAP) or a local charity. Accessing counselling privately tends to offer longer-term support, and if the woman has private health insurance, these benefits, again, are extremely useful, and sessions are managed through the counsellor by the provider.

It is important for therapists to prepare themselves, to come alongside clients who have often experienced many episodes of trauma through the loss/losses of a child, and the physical, mental, emotional and hormonal stresses that arise as a result. It is good practice, therefore, for clinicians to attend to their own life story episodes regarding loss, including generational child loss or maternal loss in childbirth. As this matter can be a taboo subject in our Black and Brown culture of origin, taking time to enquire of elders of generational knowledge, mapping out the stories and effects will prepare counsellors for the work.

Drawing on the lens of self-reflection and the therapist noticing their own internal narratives will pick up any blind spots in the intervention. Good supervision, self-reflexivity, peer groups and having their own therapy is key for containment and therapists' wellbeing. Continuing professional development (CPD) in this specialised area for all therapists working with this client group is imperative to raise the level of awareness and include cultural interventions that feel authentic for the client and their families.[18]

Counsellors working in therapy with clients with multiple losses

Clients will want to tell their stories, and for counsellors and therapists, providing a safe space is a prerequisite. Helping mothers to advocate for themselves is a good method of planning the work, which can often commence with the client taking time off work with bereavement leave after pregnancy loss. Supporting clients with some practical guidance around bereavement leave and sickness absence reduces anxiety around returning to work. In England, if a client loses a baby after 24 weeks, they are, as a minimum, entitled to statutory maternity leave. These rights are not afforded before 24 weeks. However, it is important to support the client to approach her GP to certify a period of sickness for mothers who have suffered the death of a baby at any stage of pregnancy; four weeks is not unreasonable. This can be talked through in counselling a session, as having a plan is a useful way to frame the next few weeks and months.

Pacing the sessions

Clients need to know that therapists can manage their pace, even when they themselves may not have fully understood what has been going on. Journaling is a helpful way for clients to make sense of their day-to-day experience – while they grieve, the sun still rises, and it will set, and the moon rises at sundown. Recording and making sense of their feelings is both reflective and containing with therapeutic support.[19] Therapists may also find that clients are suffering from post-traumatic stress disorder (PTSD), and it is imperative that they have the required training and experience to work with this manifestation of distress.

Holding and processing grief

With the help of talking, and journaling where appropriate, the five stages of grief and bereavement can be worked through: denial, anger, bargaining, depression and acceptance. Carefully supporting the client's entry at any stage is helpful and not prescriptive, as the process is not linear. Dependent on the client, distress may be expressed silently or through wailing, on the chair or on the floor. The client may or may not have looked at or held their baby, and may have a range of imaginations regarding how their child looked, or would look like, and this is an important part of the grief process, particularly where the client may have regrets.[20] Working alongside the culture of the client in a non-judgemental way provides an equitable acceptance, raising the therapist's own cultural awareness of their level of training and experience regarding the various expressions of distress.

Supporting mothers to advocate for themselves in preparation for the next pregnancy, or for those who are newly pregnant again

During the work with the client, she may wish to try again, or be pregnant and be understandably fearful. Connecting with a facilitative group of mothers who have experienced loss is a helpful way out of feeling isolated. Perhaps they may wish to try another hospital with specialist care and be unaware of their rights to choose their hospital facility. Pacing their feelings through other parents' stories, to include their partner in the process, is a helpful step.[21] As a Black or Brown mother to be, having images that resemble their growing child and themselves is a helpful way to connect to their identity. Due to a dearth of anatomical images of Black people in medical journals, medical illustrator Chidiebere Ibe has intentionally contributed to the inclusivity of representative images of Black people in medical books and journals.

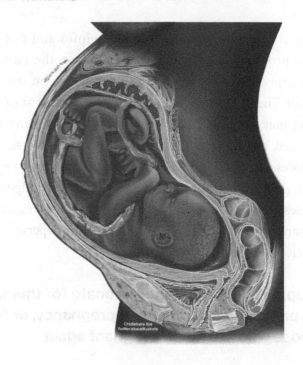

Figure 2: 'The Black fetus' illustration © Chidiebere Ibe (2021), adapted
from the original illustration © QA International (2010)

Exploring the impact of suggested high pain threshold and not feeling listened to

With images that are representative, working collaboratively with
expectant mothers is a prerequisite for good care. Pain management,
inappropriate use of examinations and instruments and the lack of
knowledge of the patient's history can cause distress and life-threatening situations. The membrane sweep (which should not be un-
dertaken after the waters have broken) – the 'normative' two-finger
examination of women often in labour – can cause extreme distress
whether administered by a male or female clinician, or without
knowledge of the mother's experience of interference, abuse or

the now outlawed 'virginity tests'. Distress can also be experienced post-pregnancy, at a mother's most vulnerable time, by a digital rectal examination without administering the recommended pain relief or being given the option to decline the procedure.

Normalising Black women in these images should change the bias in treatment. Serena Williams, a high-profile tennis player, shared her post-delivery experience in the media. Being aware of symptoms of blood clots, she alerted her medical team, who were dismissive. Williams states, 'I almost died after giving birth to my daughter...[and] was lucky to receive excellent care, but others are not so fortunate after giving birth.'[22] We must do all that we can to advocate the normality of Black and Brown people being listened to and heard, as they are often the experts of their pain threshold. Black women are often pressured to receive contraception that may not be beneficial or conducive to their emotional or physical health.[23] Advocating for the correct instrument when administering a smear test is another area that requires research.

Summary

In destigmatising counselling and support for families who have lost babies and infants and who have encountered severe distress and enduring grief systems, it is important to ensure that the effect of bias and racism in medicine, midwifery and therapeutic training and practice is not only addressed in preventative treatment, but also adheres to the cultural normative process of loss for the extended family and is incorporated into the care of the mother, father, child and extended family system. This will result in less stigma, increased openness in therapy and better outcomes in case of prolonged grief, which require containment and support culturally adaptive interventions through dignity and care.

Access to resources, and links to practitioners who can offer a supportive environment to heal, is important for ameliorating the loss of a child, or, of course, the devastating loss of a mother in childbirth. These resources must be culturally appropriate to aid recovery. The Useful Organisations and Resources listed at the end of the book will go some way to create a pathway of support and generational healing for Black and Brown families, enhance the therapist's skills and develop services.

Notes

1. www.aft.org.uk
2. www.orri-uk.com/family-therapy
3. https://hopebereavementsupport.com
4. Medforth, J., Battersby, S., Evans, M., Marsh, B. and Walker, A. (2006) *Oxford Handbook of Midwifery*. Oxford: Oxford University Press.
5. Arnold, E. (2012) *Working with Families of African Caribbean Origin: Understanding Issues around Immigration and Attachment*. London: Jessica Kingsley Publishers, pp.28–29.
6. Wall, L.L. (2020) 'The controversial Dr J. Marion Sims (1813–1833).' *International Urogynaecology Journal 31*, 7, 1299–1303. doi: 10.1007/s00192-020-04301-9.
7. Edge, D. and Rogers, A. (2005) 'Dealing with it: Black Caribbean women's response to adversity and psychological distress associated with pregnancy, childbirth, and early motherhood.' *Social Science & Medicine 61*, 1, 15–25. doi: 10.1016/j.socscimed.2004.11.047.
8. Carberry, K. (2022) Interview with Ansa Ahmed, CEO of HOPE Bereavement Support, 24 January, Leeds.
9. Edge, D. and Rogers, A. (2005).
10. Summers, H. (2021) '"I felt humiliated": Parents respond to NHS maternity care racial bias inquiry.' *The Guardian*, 13 April. www.theguardian.com/global-development/2021/apr/13/i-felt-humiliated-parents-respond-to-nhs-maternity-care-racial-bias-inquiry; Williams, S. (2018) 'Serena Williams: I almost died after giving birth to my daughter.' *Guardian Sport*, 20 February. www.theguardian.com/sport/2018/feb/20/serena-williams-childbirth-health-daughter-tennis
11. MBRRACE-UK (Mothers and Babies: Reducing Risk through Audits and Confidential Enquires across the UK) (2020) www.npeu.ox.ac.uk/mbrrace-uk
12. Rowe, H. and Hawkey, A.J. (2020) 'Miscarriage.' In J.M. Usher, J.C. Chrisler and J. Perz (eds) *Routledge International Handbook of Women's Sexual and Reproductive Health* (pp.297–299). Abingdon: Routledge.
13. Edge, D. and Rogers, A. (2005).
14. Hill, M. (7 February 2023) Gloucester mother died after post-birth treatment delay. BBC News retrieved https://www.bbc.co.uk/news/uk-england-gloucestershire-64496514 Howard, J. (22 February 2020) When women die in childbirth, these are the fathers left behind. CNN news retrieved https://edition.cnn.com/2020/02/21/health/maternal-mortality-fathers-grief/index.html

15. Carberry, K. (2022) Interview with Ansa Ahmed, CEO of HOPE Bereavement Support, 24 January, Leeds.

16. Royal College of Obstetricians and Gynaecologist (2020) Molar pregnancy and gestational trophoblastic disease. https://www.rcog.org.uk/for-the-public/browse-our-patient-information/molar-pregnancy-and-gestational-trophoblastic-disease

17. Cacciatore, J. and Weiber Lens, J. (2020) 'The Ultimate in Women's Labor. Stillbirth and Grieving.' In J.M. Usher, J.C. Chrisler and J. Perz (eds) *Routledge International Handbook of Women's Sexual and Reproductive Health* (pp.310–313). Abingdon: Routledge.

18. Ryde, J. (2009) *Being White in the Helping Professions: Developing Effective Intercultural Awareness.* London: Jessica Kingsley Publishers.

19. Clarke-Coates, Z. (2020) *The Baby Loss Guide: Practical and Compassionate Support with a Day-by-Day Resource to Navigate the Path of Grief.* London: Orion Spring, pp.261–381.

20. Moulder, C. (1998) *Understanding Pregnancy Loss: Perspectives and Issues in Care.* Basingstoke: Macmillan, pp.174–177.

21. Clarke-Coates, Z. (2020) *The Baby Loss Guide: Practical and Compassionate Support with a Day-by-Day Resource to Navigate the Path of Grief.* London: Orion Spring, pp.261–381.

22. Williams, S. (2018) 'Serena Williams: I almost died after giving birth to my daughter.' *Guardian Sport,* 20 February. www.theguardian.com/sport/2018/feb/20/serena-williams-childbirth-health-daughter-tennis

23. Becker, D. and Tsui, A.O. (2008) 'Reproductive health service preferences and perceptions of quality among low-income women: racial, ethnic and language group difference.' *Perspective on Sexual and Reproductive Health 40,* 4, 202–211, p.208.

Remember Me

Amanda Inniss

Shed no tear for me, for I am gone beyond the clouds My life on earth
*   was all too fleeting,*
You made each moment count

Remember me with joy
Remember me in song

I am far away in the distance, another universe

I am so glad for the time we spent together,

Here on earth

Raise your head with fondness,
And wipe away your tears
You shall never be lonely, for I shall always be near

And as the years roll by, the pain and the hurt will ease Remember
*   each time to smile*
When you remember me.

15 Suicide in the Shadows of Grenfell

Sister Isis Amlak

Isis stands as an Afrikan Queen Mother Warrior first and foremost; she is an Afrikan woman of the Yoruba nation, born in Trinidad and Tobago. Isis has resided and worked in the North Kensington area for nearly 35 years, in both paid and voluntary roles. She has provided advocacy, mental health, police monitoring and other services to minoritised and racialised communities, while also contributing to local democracy and serving on various boards and networks. Isis is a Pan-Afrikanist, and a seasoned activist and campaigner for racial and social justice and reparatory justice for the enslavement of Afrikans. Isis holds an MA in Black British Writing.

Note: Suicide is the act of intentionally ending your life. If you're reading this and you have, or have had, thoughts about taking your own life, it's important you ask someone for help. It's probably difficult for you to see at this time, but you are not alone and you are not beyond help.

By the time you read this I will have passed. I need to let you know that there is nothing you could have done to stop this from happening... The Grenfell Tower fire has affected me badly. I had hoped the worst would be over, but 17 months after I still suffer from acute anxiety. I really don't know why it has affected me so badly, but it isn't a life worth living.

Those words echoed in my ears as I heard the extract of the suicide note read at the inquest of my friend and Sista, Amanda Beckles. The revelation that the Grenfell Tower fire had played a role in circumstances that led to Amanda taking her life is not a shock if you know the North Kensington community and felt the effects of the preventable deaths of at least 72 people who were our families, friends and neighbours. Amanda died by suicide on 13th December 2019.

Amanda Beckles was a phenomenal woman in the truest sense of those words. She was 52 and lived a short walk from the Tower. Amanda was a critical thinker and an intellectual – engaging, entertaining and funny. She was involved in many initiatives that set out to support, capacity-build and empower marginalised communities, particularly Women of Afrikan Heritage. Amanda took immense pride in her history, culture and identity. She was one of the founding members of the One Voice Community Collective, a movement to advance the socio-economic interest of People from the African diaspora, and of the Sistas' Creative Circle™ based in West London, a collective of Women of Afrikan Heritage.

Amanda was severely traumatised by the Grenfell Tower fire and, like so many others who lived close to the Tower, she was angry about the atrocity that she saw as being the direct result of negligence, neglect and corruption, and considered it an act of institutional murder.

The Royal Borough of Kensington and Chelsea (RBKC) is an extremely 'divided borough'. The socio-political history of RBKC legitimately earns it the eponymous title of 'a tale of two cities'. Billionaires and the obscenely rich live next-door, opposite or around the corner from impoverished, disenfranchised people struggling to make ends meet. In the Borough of Westminster, the wellbeing scores for happiness were higher than the London average, while in Kensington and Chelsea they were lower than average.[1]

Seen through a public health lens, it was a disaster waiting to happen given the stark health inequalities that existed, as the JSNA report also stated that the rates of depression and prevalence of serious mental health illness were higher than the London average and that there were also higher rates of households in temporary accommodation.

The social housing stock run by the tenant management organisation (TMO) has been reported in the press as being mismanaged and starved of investment – an example of the phrase 'outsourcing kills'.

Amanda was a staunch grass-roots community organiser, as well as an academic – she held a BA in Philosophy, an MA in African Studies and an MSC in Environmental Management for Business. In response to the fire, among other things, she founded the Grenfell Tower Community Monitoring Project (GTCMP), the main aim being to 'hold the Conservative-run Royal Borough of Kensington and Chelsea Council to account in regard to housing and support services provided to the communities affected by the fire'.

Through the GTCMP Amanda ran Chat Back™ discussion sessions as a way of getting communities talking to and supporting each other, enabling the voices of all those affected to be heard, and particularly those who found it more difficult to be heard. Amanda spoke out at meetings and in the media, raising many criticisms of the government and local authority over the fire and what she saw as their total lack of empathy for those suffering its impact. She was determined that the RBKC Council should be held to account.

The previous year I had been in shock to learn of the death, by suicide, of my friend Tim Burke who, like Amanda, had been a community activist profoundly affected by the fire. A filmmaker, writer and agent provocateur, Tim set up the legendary Portobello Pop Up cinema, which was built using local recycled material, with a 30ft screen. On the morning of the fire, he was on the ground with the rest of us, devastated and dazed, but getting on with aiding our community.

Tim said that it was 'a terrible sight, every inch of space taken by people silently sitting, saying nothing, in the clothes they had escaped in, reeking of smoke...' Tim campaigned against the discrimination faced by the North Kensington community, including fighting to save Portobello Market from developers, and crusading for the locals to reclaim their community space beneath the Westway.

For all their strengths and triumphs, Amanda and Tim were also vulnerable people with histories of depression caught up in an unprecedentedly traumatic situation. Amanda had reported being anxious about her mental health and was experiencing financial difficulties. The inquest heard that her medical records showed she was exhibiting signs of post-traumatic stress disorder (PTSD), that her savings were running out and she had to apply for welfare benefits, and that she was at risk of eviction from her home. Grenfell had affected her badly. At Tim's funeral several of his friends also recalled how badly Grenfell had affected him.

In December 2017 there were reports of multiple suicides. The *Mirror* reported: 'Exclusive: 24 suicide attempts by Grenfell survivors or witnesses since blaze which killed 71 residents... The shocking figure emerged as more than 100 families who lived in the tower block prepare to spend Christmas Day in hotels and other temporary digs.'[2] SOS Silence of Suicide[3] founder Yvette Greenway told the BBC's Victoria Derbyshire programme that there had been at least 20, and that number was based on conversations with residents.[4]

Suicidal feelings can be confusing, frightening and complicated. They can range from having general thoughts about not wanting to be here to making a plan about how and when you could end your life. You might feel less like you want to die, and more that you want the pain to stop. Anecdotally, locals were hearing of many suicide attempts connected to the impact of the fire and the after-effects, in the wake of which we strongly feel that the RBKC

Council failed to respond to our North Kensington community appropriately and compassionately.

In 2020 it was reported that Dr Deborah Lamont, a university lecturer who had been part of an emergency response team at Grenfell, and labelled by the press a 'Grenfell Hero', had died by suicide. Of her experience at the scene of the fire she said,

> the atmosphere was heavy in the aftermath of the fire and a lot of the time the area was still dark with smoke... It was emotionally challenging for me but I was grateful for the opportunity to help them and I am not likely to forget the scenes I saw but I would volunteer again in a heartbeat because that's the reason I joined up.[5]

The NHS recovery unit's response to the fire was said to be the biggest of its kind in Europe, and it was reported that more than £10 million was spent on mental health support services and treatment for those affected.[6] In the year after the fire, 2674 adults and 463 children were screened for symptoms of post-traumatic stress disorder (PTSD). The St Charles Centre for Health and Wellbeing opened in Ladbroke Grove so that those affected could be treated in dedicated therapy suites. Yet despite the many commitments made by the borough and other government agencies, conditions for many of the survivors and other displaced residents remained intolerable, as this highlights:

> One of our clients was initially moved into a hotel and then temporary accommodation after the fire. She was finally moved into permanent housing in February 2019 where there were excessive noise issues from the road and neighbours. She has also been unable to open the windows as they are too heavy, and this means that there is no ventilation. Condensation and mould have been a significant problem because of this. Our client

has detailed how this has significantly damaged her mental health and her ability to feel settled. It was later confirmed that the damp and structural issues were far worse than previously thought, and the living conditions were considered unsafe. However, our client has been waiting for an extensive period of time to be rehoused and has informed us that she has been close to suicide during this time. There are reports of elevated levels of PTSD and suicide rates and low levels of culturally relevant therapeutic interventions post-the Grenfell fire.[7]

The scale of that trauma – impossible to fathom even among those who escaped from the Tower or lost loved ones – has been amplified by the fact that many people who lived in the vicinity of Grenfell had, in childhood, fled from conflict or terror. For those one-time refugees, the unavoidable sight of the inferno, and the chaos and displacement that ensued, made all sorts of buried nightmares resurface.

PTSD UK estimates that about 50–70 per cent of people will experience a traumatic event in their lifetime.[8] There is a high population-level burden of PTSD associated with the unexpected death of a loved one, which highlights the need to better understand risk factors such as exposure to traumatic events to effectively prevent suicidality and suicide risk. There is substantial evidence that most people receiving treatment for mental health issues have had some form of trauma, and that trauma places people at a higher risk for mental health issues such as depression and addiction. People who have experienced trauma are also at a greater risk for suicide.

Professor Louis Appleby, the NHS's national lead on suicide prevention, published a 2020 review, *Suicide Safety in North Kensington*,[9] which noted that:

- Suicide rates have not risen as a result of the Grenfell fire.

- However, in a small number of individual suicides, the fire is likely to have contributed.
- The widespread concern about suicide is important in its own right as it reflects a feeling of insecurity and a belief that the distress of individuals is not fully heard.

Professor Appleby made it clear that suicide prevention needed to do more than be based on numbers. In his report, *Suicide Prevention Following the Grenfell Fire*,[10] he set out some key principles: that suicide prevention includes ensuring the community's 'psychological safety'; all local leaders and frontline agencies should sign up to it; it should be at the front of any local plans for recovery; children and young people should take priority; and, high-quality data is essential. He also reported that the suicide prevention measures as a response to Grenfell and Covid-19 be brought together, with their central common themes of inequality, ethnicity and stigma.

During the Grenfell Inquiry Professor Appleby reaffirmed that the trauma had hit hard, and the inquiry process was proving very painful for those affected by the atrocity. Suicide safety and prevention is an ongoing issue that fits in line with the multi-agency agenda of increasing awareness of mental health and wellbeing, combating stigmatisation and shame across various community groups, and improving knowledge about self-care and knowledge of and access to services. Having spoken with many of the bereaved – relatives and survivors as well as other members of the community – about their experiences, he said that 'More must be done to help protect Grenfell community from suicide'.[11] We need to talk about suicide to stop more lives being lost.

Suicides are deemed a major public health problem, and, according to the 2022 Samaritans *Ethnicity and Suicide* report,[12] in the UK there is evidence of racial disparities in the data mainly because information on ethnicity has not been routinely collected, there is misclassification and underreporting. A June 2021 newspaper article titled 'The real reason why Black men are most at risk of suicide' notes that the suicide rates for men recently reached an all-time high in England and Wales, with young men of Afrikan heritage more at risk of taking their lives than White men.[13]

Suicide is the single biggest killer of men under the age of 50, with three quarters of deaths from suicide being men.[14] In the general population the lifetime prevalence of suicidality has been reported as 1 in 5 people having suicide ideation, 1 in 14 people self-harming and 1 in 15 people making suicide attempts.[15] These UK rates are alarming, and there is a desperate need to increase awareness of the risk factors associated with suicidality such as suicidal thoughts, suicidal self-harm and suicide attempts. Evidentially there is also an association between PTSD and suicidality.

Most people conceive of suicide as being caused solely by severe mental illness, and in many cases, a mood disorder or other diagnosable psychological condition will play a significant role. But many people who display no signs of depression, substance use disorder, bipolar disorder or any other mental illness die by suicide too. While these deaths are often shocking and confusing to their loved ones, the individual's decision to take their own life may be attributable to one or several of a wide range of physical or socio-cultural factors.

An article published in *Suicide and Life-Threatening Behavior* found that daily discrimination influences depression and suicidal ideation: 'These findings demonstrate that for Black adults, perceived discrimination serves as a sufficiently painful and provocative experience that is directly associated with higher capability to overcome one's inherent fear of death and an increased capacity for self-harm'.[16] This is hardly surprising considering that many markers associated with suicide and suicidality align with factors emanating from socio-economic deprivation, experiences of discrimination, exclusion and feeling unsafe, and the link between long-standing health inequalities and racism.

The impact of suicide is felt far and wide, and it is said that for every person who dies by suicide, there are at least ten people who are directly affected, but that number does not take account of those who belong to communities that have had to come together and unify themselves for a common cause – communities like those that Amanda was a key part of that came together to fight against systemic racism and health inequalities.

Amanda's untimely passing reflects the long and difficult history that people of Afrikan heritage experience of the mental health system. This, itself, is part of a broader struggle with structural racism that people of Afrikan heritage contend with to this day.

Notes

1. JSNA (Joint Strategic Needs Assessment) (2019) 'Mental health and wellbeing JSNA.' May. www.jsna.info/document/mental-health-and-wellbeing-jsna

2. Hill, P. (2017) '24 suicide attempts by Grenfell survivors or witnesses since blaze which killed 71 residents.' *Mirror*, 23 December. www.mirror.co.uk/news/uk-news/tragedy-24-suicide-attempts-grenfell-11746403

3. https://sossilenceofsuicide.org

4. BBC News (2017) 'Grenfell Tower: "Twenty suicide attempts" since fire.' 5 September. www.bbc.co.uk/news/uk-41148877

5. Corbishley, S. (2020) 'Hero Grenfell doctor found hanged hours after sending text saying "it's my time".' *Metro*, 16 January. https://metro.co.uk/2020/01/16/hero-grenfell-doctor-found-hanged-hours-sending-text-saying-time-12071695

6. Adams, T. (2019) 'The hidden mental-health legacy of Grenfell Tower.' *The Guardian*, 9 June. www.theguardian.com/uk-news/2019/jun/09/hidden-mental-health-legacy-grenfell-disaster

7. Sennik, B. (2022) '"It's that internal struggle": Grenfell residents lived experience of psychological distress, post-fire, 14-06-17. An interpretative phenomenological analysis.' Prof. Doc. Thesis, University of East London School of Psychology. https://doi.org/10.15123/uel.8w525

8. www.ptsduk.org/what-is-ptsd/ptsd-explained

9. Central and North West London NHS Foundation Trust (2020) *Suicide Safety in North Kensington: Updates on Recommendations from Prof Louis Appleby.* 9 April. https://rbkc.moderngov.co.uk/Committees/Data/Adult%20Social%20Care%20&%20Health%20Select%20Committee/202104191830/Agenda/A4%20-%20CNWL%20Appleby%20Report%20Reccommendations.pdf

10. Central and North West London NHS Foundation Trust (2020) 'Report calls for "suicide

safety" in North Kensington.' 18 September. www.cnwl.nhs.uk/news/report-calls-suicide-safety-north-kensington

11. Central and North West London NHS Foundation Trust (2020) 'Report calls for "suicide safety" in North Kensington.' 18 September. www.cnwl.nhs.uk/news/report-calls-suicide-safety-north-kensington

12. Samaritans (2022) *Ethnicity and Suicide.* Samaritans Policy Position, July. https://media.samaritans.org/documents/Ethnicity_and_suicide_July_2022.pdf

13. Morris, N. (2021) 'The real reason why Black men are most at risk of suicide.' *Metro*, 7 June. https://metro.co.uk/2021/06/07/a-looming-crisis-why-black-men-are-most-at-risk-of-suicide-14621250

14. www.statista.com/statistics/289102/suicide-rate-in-the-united-kingdom-uk-by-age

15. https://www.mind.org.uk/information-support/types-of-mental-health-problems/mental-health-facts-and-statistics/

16. Brooks, J.R., Hong, J.H., Cheref, S. and Walker, R.L. (2020) 'Capability for suicide: Discrimination as a painful and provocative event.' *Suicide and Life-Threatening Behavior 50*, 6, 1173–80. https://doi.org/10.1111/sltb.12671

16 The Artist in Grenfell

Damel Carayol

*Damel is a Gambian-born UK resident. Painter, musician and poet —
essentially an artist. Visually he is engaged in portraiture through media
and material that often breaks the rules. His core passion, he finds, is to exalt
echoes of 'smaller' voices, and so deliver a better understanding of 'who we
are as a oneness'.*

In West Africa, in The Gambia in particular, where I have experience,
death, burial and grief are, in essence, causes for the affirmations
of a 'oneness' of family, belonging and togetherness. The ultimate
respect is paid to the passing of a soul. For it is a strongly held belief
and tradition that a soul becomes an ancestor. Much is owed to our
ancestors for their connection with and guidance of us here, in the
physical world, in close tangent with our connection and hopeful
expectation of the Creator Him or Herself.

Wednesday 14th June 2017 saw the tragedy of the devastating
fire at Grenfell Tower in North Kensington, West London. I received
a phone call shortly after midnight from the wife of my very close
cousin Gabriel Mendy. She was in the UK on a short visit from The
Gambia, where she and her immediate family live, and was due to
return on the Friday. 'Damel, turn the TV on' she said, and I did.

The sight was unbelievable – we were hearing and apparently
seeing Grenfell Tower. I knew the building and its name, but for
some reason it didn't connect with me that this was the same place
I was looking at. My cousin's wife knew the building intimately.

She and her husband had previously stayed there for some months. Their son was, in fact, born while they were staying there with another cousin, Mary Mendy, and her daughter (and my niece), Khadija Saye. Mary was Gabriel's sister.

'Grenfell Tower' one of us said, and that was all that was said.

As it slowly, unbelievably, sank in that this was the Grenfell Tower we knew, my thought went straight to the fact that Mary and Khadija lived on a high floor level. This was a 24-storey block, and Mary and Khadija had previously moved from the top to the 20th floor.

According to one of the first eyewitnesses interviewed, the building was engulfed in flames in a matter of a few minutes. This resulted from a fridge fire on the 4th floor. How could Mary and Khadija, or anyone else, escape from this horrific inferno? I was in a state of feeling what it must be like to be suspended in time, or perhaps being in a vacuum of incomprehension. I didn't know the questions much less the answers to anything! It was just pain and grief, mixed with deep despair and helplessness.

I knew we both were crying continuously and uncontrollably through the whole watching until we both put the phone down and continued to watch and weep alone.

The next two days seemed to be the longest. It was more like noticing the minutes and the hours rather than the days. I don't remember if I slept, or for how long. All the family, here in the UK, The Gambia, Senegal and the USA were in painful communication, and I, along with my cousin Gabriel's wife, were in hourly contact with another niece who had grown up closely with Khadija. She was going from hospital to hospital – St Mary's to St Thomas' to St George's to St Charles' – trying to see if Mary and Khadija had been admitted. Our hope was strong. Sense should have told us that to survive from the 20th floor in that raging fire would have been very difficult, but hope that they were both in a hospital somewhere far outweighed any consideration of 'making sense'.

Khadija's father had also been searching. In fact, signs saying 'Lost' with pictures of family members, loved ones and neighbours were all over the community, with phone numbers and messages left on lamp posts, shops, walls and fences, along with candles and flowers. Hope that the 'Lost' would sooner or later be found, alive.

I couldn't go to the building. I hadn't yet found the courage to go to the area. It was an area I knew so well; just a quarter of a mile from Latimer Road Station where Grenfell Tower stood was the first home I had in London on arrival from The Gambia aged nine. I had joined my parents and we lived at Oxford Gardens. Latimer Road was my local station and Ladbroke Grove my High Street.

On the morning of Friday 16th June, after continuously listening to the TV and radio and reliving the pain and anger, I tuned into James O'Brien's 10 am radio show on LBC. At 10:30, he read out a report on the recent 'refurbishment' of Grenfell Tower – one of four high-rise blocks set in the middle of a part of the Royal Borough where houses and apartments sold for multiples of millions of pounds. The report spoke of how the building was now seen to be 'aesthetically pleasing' when viewed from the West of the Borough, and from the South and the East. Word had been that these blocks were a blight on an affluent landscape, eyesores that affected property prices. This report tipped me over the edge and my growing anger turned into absolute rage as it confirmed to me that this prettying-up was definitely done for the onlooker and not the residents.

I was home alone. A large canvas remained in my living room – the only one left following a year-long painting project from May 2016 to May 2017 I had completed. For some reason I had previously drawn grid lines on it and was intending for it to be a painting to make a statement about Donald Trump. However, now, swearing, stomping and sweating, I grabbed the canvas, brushes, any paint I could find – mainly black gloss, black sprays, silver – and on my new rug on the living room floor I poured out as much of my anger as I could onto the canvas. I had taken a quick photo using my phone of the burnt-out Tower as shown on the TV and referred to this to paint. My thought was 'Eye-sore' and my feeling 'The Final Straw'.

Following on from years of pain, protest, Poll Tax riots, strikes, the Iraq war and austerity measures, and a diminishing belief that political power is actually lent to politicians by the People, I felt that Grenfell was a deafening reminder to the whole world to stop and think again – how can we organise our societies? Grenfell was a loud wake-up call for the world.

I propped up the work and decided to call it 'Eye-sore. The Final Straw!!' Seeing my cousin's wife off at the airport, I felt it meaningful for her to be the first to see 'Eye-sore. The Final Straw!!' I had completed the painting in five or six non-stop hours. Previous completions had taken up to three months.

That evening I was able to go to Latimer Road. Perhaps the visceral outpouring of the painting had eased me a little, enough that I was able to go out. I counted the floors to Mary and Khadija's floor, and now feared the worst. Hundreds upon hundreds of people were there, including many of my own family. The Mendy family, the Senghores, Turpins, Hardings and N'jies. We are all related, we were all there. Some had flown in from the USA and from The Gambia with hope remaining strong in the 'Lost' signs everywhere, for this 'lost' meant not found, as opposed to lost and gone forever.

Near where we'd put up a Gambian flag was an A4 photocopy of a photo of a boy with children's handwriting on it. It read, 'We will fight for you', 'We will never forget you' and 'I'm so sorry'.

It was here I first learned about Yahya Hashim, a 12-year-old boy who had died in the fire, by a lady who screamed out 'No, not him too!' She went on to explain how intellectually smart Yahya was, studying for his GCSEs years ahead of time. Yahya Hashim became the second painting I would create connected to Grenfell. He and another four members of his family, including Firdaws Hashim, perished in the fire. It was some days after that we found out that Mary and Khadija had been found, but had not made it out.

So how do we deal with grief? My grief was now multiplying and my anger intensifying due to the loss of my family members and the many other families I was meeting and getting to know. All of us suffering the same.

Our journey was inextricably linked by the Grenfell tragedy and why it happened, and I would become very closely connected to them in a long fight for justice and recognition of causes, and a further fight to prevent it recurring. I travelled to many meetings and events with my cousin Clarrie Mendy, who has since passed.

My view is that we, as men, are generally socialised to 'be strong' and not to give in to emotions. I don't think that this is a phenomenon of nature but rather learned behaviour. I had learned many years prior and by deduction that we all have emotions for very good reasons. We must connect with them and allow them if not free reign, at least to be expressed. It truly is damaging to suppress or bottle up emotions that need to be expressed.

I had not previously heard or thought of art as therapy, or as a form of healing, and in the 13 pieces I went on to create about Grenfell, I wasn't considering their creation as being cathartic. I was driven to do these, and it is only in hindsight, and in writing here, that it now dawns on me that this was and is a most valuable form of expression of feelings and emotions. Guided? Yes!! By our ancestors? Yes!!

Khadija was an artist and a photographer whose star was bright and rising. She and her mother, along with both my parents, have joined our ancestors. My feeling that I have to do what I can for her and for them is strong in me, and I am sure they spur me on and guide me. I live by that conviction daily.

Being in the UK, I have a strong sense of duty to fight the cause for justice in the face of the devastating failures that led up to the fire – for my family abroad, for my cousins Gabriel and Anna as

Mary's brother and sister, and for the whole family. Equally for all the families of all the passed relatives I have come to know and have worked with.

It is said that 'the devil finds work for idle hands or minds'. A strong statement. In my view, a lack of talking, sharing and expressing of grief can equally be finding work for future uncontrolled and perhaps dangerous outbursts arising from internal struggle and strain. I did receive counselling during the period, something I had never before put much thought in, but now I realised the value of it.

Unfortunately, not everyone has the closeness of family and friends to express their grief, emotions and anger safely and freely. I know I am blessed to have very close friends as well as family. What is more, I have my creativity, which is driven by intense and visceral feelings, observations and an absolute need to make statements to try to better our world.

I believe that opportunities to just let it out should be taken by those who may not find it so easy in the relationships and associations that are around them. We, as people, and men in particular, need to encourage ourselves and other men around us to 'talk'. Share inner feelings, thoughts and fears. That is what I decided to do many years ago and it helps me a great deal. By taking this course of action honestly and without fear, male friends who are just waiting for one person to spark these conversations will join in the healing journey. Your relationship can then be on a deeper level through sharing experiences.

The artworks I've done on and for Grenfell have travelled around the world and have been powerfully displayed in exhibitions and theatre performances. 'Eye-sore' was first shown at an anniversary celebration of the Empire Windrush's first sailing to the UK from the Caribbean, where I spoke of the Grenfell tragedy. It has travelled with me to many talks, from political party meetings to memorial services, to the Houses of Parliament.

In 2018 a print copy was handed to then Prime Minister Theresa

May and hung in No. 10 Downing Street. Another copy was hung in the Grenfell Tower Inquiry room from the outset, and is in the gifted ownership of Michael Mansfield QC and theatre director Nicolas Kent. As I write in 2022, it is less than ten days to the fifth anniversary of the fire. I will be displaying the painting at Westminster Abbey where a memorial service is being held, all reminders of what happened and why we must, as a country and as leaders strive for the situation to be remedied and fixed for current and future generations.

Writing this has given me an additional focus and outlet. The pain and anger does not dissipate; it carries on as we continue to find out more and more about how rotten some decisions and organisational and political actions and inactions have been.

But altogether, along with the people here and the departed who I have mentioned, we make up what some simply term as 'support'. We all need it. Any plant or building or ailing relationship can collapse without support. If support doesn't find us, we need to look for it.

The answers are within us; they are around us. We must seek to find, believe that we can, and let hope and trust in, and project inner strength outwards.

Back to the Black

Amanda Inniss

I don't know why some people walk around
Thinking they better than some
We are all the made from the same flesh and bone
We all have the same red blood

And it's back to the black earth we all going
Cause that's where we call come from
Rich man, poor man, beggar and a teef
All ah we gone pass out, and be buried underneath

So, whilst we are on this good and green earth,

Let's all unite, come together as one,
Cause stress for nobody,
And everybody have some fun!

Cause back to the black earth we all going
Cause that's where we call come from
Rich man, poor man, beggar and a teef
All ah we gone pass out, and be buried underneath

I don't know why some rich folk think, nobody can touch them

Doing all the evil they can,
Sooner or later they gonna need their fellow man

Big bank accounts make them forget,
But when that final hour is upon them
It's then they realise, nobody is an island

Nobody is superhuman.
Cause back to the black earth we all going
Cause that's where we call come from
Rich man, poor man, beggar and a teef
All ah we gone pass out, and be buried underneath

I don't know why some people always make a commotion,

Stirring up nuff trouble, finding fault in everything they see,

Deep down, those people, are just not truly happy

Cause if they were happy, they would be celebrating, Enjoying and
*   having fun*
Instead of walking around and talking and putting their mouth
*   everywhere it don't even belong!*
Yes, its back to the black earth we all going,
Cause that's where we call come from
Rich man, poor man, beggar and a teef
All ah we gone pass out, and be buried underneath

So please do your best to be loving,
You only have one life, so they say
Spread a little joy, make someone happy,
Smile and live your life the right way
Cause back to the black earth we all going
Cause that's where we call come from
Rich man poor man, beggar and a teef
All ah we gone pass out, and be buried underneath.

17 Black Don't Crack or Does It: The Home Office Scandal

Patrick Vernon

Patrick is chair of Birmingham and Solihull Integrated Care System (ICS), which commissions healthcare for a population of 1.2 million people, and is also chair of Walsall Together health partnership. He is a patron of ACCI (African Caribbean Community Initiative),[1] a long-established Black mental health charity, and of Santé Refugee Mental Heath Access Project.[2] He is also an independent adviser on equality, diversity and inclusion (EDI) for the Crown Prosecution Service. Patrick has been helping to expose the Home Office Windrush Scandal since 2018 in one of the first online petitions calling for an amnesty for the Windrush Generation. He is a broadcaster, public speaker and EDI advocate, and writes blogs and articles for the national and international media on healthcare, mental health, cultural heritage and race.

In April 2018 the public in the UK, and indeed the whole world, was exposed to what we now know as the Windrush scandal. That scandal involved the stripping away of the citizenship rights of those who came to Britain, particularly in the period between 1948 and the early 1970s. Colonies in the Caribbean and Africa were part of the British Empire, according to the 1948 British Nationality Act, which meant that dependent children travelling on their parents', aunts', uncles' and other family members' passports had the same status and citizenship of anyone who was born in the UK. They came from countries that were invaded and colonised by the British, and therefore became British subjects. Yet, successive legislation over the last 50 years has eroded those rights.[3]

This erosion has not just affected those considered the Windrush Generation, but also those who arrived in the 1940s, 1950s, 1960s and early 1970s from the Caribbean, as well as other Commonwealth nationals and migrants.

As a nation, the UK moved into an even more toxic environment with the 2014 Immigration Act, which featured measures designed to create a 'hostile environment' for people in the UK without valid leave. The policy's main focus was to deter people coming to the UK, and to use fear and intimidation to force people from Black and racialised communities to voluntarily leave with a one-way ticket of reparation – a vision that the Far Right have been campaigning for since the early days of the colour bar.

It is now clear from the *Windrush Lessons Learned Review* that the Windrush scandal was linked directly to the 'hostile environment' policy and previous immigration legislation over the last 50 years – dating back to Enoch Powell's 'Rivers of Blood' speech in 1968, which influenced the 1968 Commonwealth Immigrants Act.[4] The Windrush scandal, or more appropriately the Home Office scandal, has caused considerable grief for so many families around us – and Black people have begun to crack. Many who were young adults and children when they arrived in the UK are now at retirement age – between their 50s and 80s – but they have no documented evidence of their citizenship. Most of them either did not acquire a passport because holidays abroad were not common back then; did not apply for naturalisation because they didn't know that they had to; or found it difficult to prove when they had come to the

UK because, in some instances, records such as landing cards had been destroyed over time.

Previously, the 1948 Nationality Act had absolved them from needing to prove that they were British, but policies designed to create a 'hostile environment' forced them into a situation where they suddenly became undocumented migrants. They had to prove that they were British, or they were deemed to be illegal immigrants. The policy strategy was hostile by name and hostile by nature!

Many thousands of mainly African and Caribbean people were subject to the onslaught of that 'hostile environment' policy strategy, and some volunteered to go back to their country of birth. There were instances of people who had been on holiday abroad being refused entry back to the UK, others were deported, and some spent considerable time in detention centres. But the reality is that the vast majority of those who could not prove their citizenship ended up losing their jobs and their homes, and access to pension rights and to NHS healthcare, even though they had been paying National Insurance contributions for well over 40 years.[5]

But those were not the only challenges they were facing. They say 'Black don't crack', but the constant pressure of having to prove citizenship to the Home Office had a serious impact on people's mental and physical wellbeing, and the first known case in the media was that of Dexter Bristol.[6]

Dexter was of Grenadian heritage and was caught in the frustrating system of having to prove his British citizenship despite having lived in the UK since he was eight years old. Because of the way the system was set up back in the 1950s, Dexter travelled to the UK in 1968 as a dependent on his mother's Grenadian British subject passport, and so he did not have his own citizenship documentation. Even though it was obvious why he didn't have it, his inability to prove his citizenship led to him being dismissed from his job and losing his right to benefits. Dexter's resilience cracked and sadly, in March 2018, he was found dead outside his home. He died a broken man.

I got to know Dexter's mother, and that encounter led to us starting GoFundMe campaigns to cover the funeral costs of family members who had lost loved ones due to the Windrush scandal. Thankfully, the campaign raised sufficient money for Dexter's funeral costs, and he had a fitting tribute. I empathised with Dexter's traumas, and felt honoured to be able to say a few words at his funeral. He was buried in South London, in the country that had tried so desperately hard to get rid of him.

In September 2019, Sarah O'Connor, aged 57, died of a stress-related illness. I met Sarah because of our mutual involvement in campaigning for justice. She regularly appeared on TV, was at the Houses of Parliament, and spoke at Windrush events. Sarah was always honest about the impact it was having on her mental health, and how stressful she found the entire process of having to retrospectively prove her entitlement to citizenship. Eventually, it took its toll, and the saddest part of Sarah's case is that she had received her citizenship certificate from Barking and Dagenham Council just before her passing.[7]

Sarah's funeral costs were paid for with funds raised by the community, and so she was able to have a proper funeral and burial. She had been under a lot of stress and tremendous pressure, and had become financially dependent on her children. The system prevented her from accessing any benefits, and at that time the government had not yet worked out what the Windrush Compensation Scheme should look like and how it would be administered, and nor did they make any provisions for interim payments to help those affected.

Theresa May did apologise, but no real financial efforts were being made to support any of those affected by the Windrush scandal until the scheme was launched in April 2019,[8] and even then, making a claim was not straightforward.[9]

For me, the biggest impact of the Windrush catastrophe was the death of Paulette Wilson, because I had got to know her and her daughter Natalie very well. Paulette arrived in the UK at the age of ten in 1968 and lived in Wolverhampton, which is ironically the same year that Enoch Powell made his infamous and emotive 'Rivers of Blood' speech, giving an apocalyptic vision of a Britain of 'violence and mayhem'. He said that Britain as a nation must be mad to take in its dependents, ignoring the fact that it was Britain that had gone into the Caribbean and Africa uninvited and unwelcomed, and colonising the inhabitants. He likened Britain taking in dependents to 'heaping up its own funeral pyre', and unfortunately that hostility towards people from the Caribbean and Africa is reflected in the structural racism that continues to exist in society today.

After living in Wolverhampton, Paulette moved to London, to the Ladbroke Grove community of North Kensington. She absolutely loved life, and used to party and rave at the Tabernacle, a well-known cultural community centre in Notting Hill, which was one of her favourite haunts. As part of her retirement she moved back to Wolverhampton. A lot of people from the Midlands have that natural yearning to go back home to the Midlands or to the north of England after years living in London, but Paulette's move was not the joyful, peaceful retirement she had planned.

Not long after the move, she started receiving letters from the Home Office about her immigration status, deeming her an illegal immigrant even though she had lived in the UK since 1968. She paid her taxes for 34 years working as a cook, and yet her benefits and access to healthcare were stopped. Eventually Paulette was arrested because of her immigration status, and sent to the Yarl's Wood detention centre even though she had not been to Jamaica since she had left as a child.

Thankfully, with the intervention of the local immigration advice centre and the local MP at the time, Paulette was eventually released.[10] That spurred her on to tell her story, and she also let others know the impact the experience of the Windrush scandal had had on her mental health. Her resilience was cracking because of the trauma and anguish she was going through, but along with many others affected by the Windrush scandal, she campaigned vigorously, and I am honoured to have known her and supported her in her quest for justice.

In the summer of 2020, during the cessation of the Covid-19 lockdown, I decided that a group of us should go to Number 10 Downing Street to present a petition.[11] I wanted to highlight the government's failure to implement the *Windrush Lessons Learned Review*, a report by Wendy Williams commissioned to explore the circumstances that led to the Windrush scandal, which was published in March 2020.[12]

That petition had over 140,000 signatures, and so the weekend before the 2020 Windrush Day on 22 June, a group including Anthony Bryan, Elwaldo Romeo, Michael Braithwaite, Paulette Wilson, her daughter Natalie, Glenda Caesar (people who were directly affected by the Windrush scandal), Satbir Singh (CEO of the Joint Council for the Welfare of Immigrants) and myself, turned up with our petition and placards for justice. All the major TV companies were present – the BBC, ITV, Channel 4 and Channel 5 – to witness us present the petition to Boris Johnson, and the campaign dominated news feed throughout the entire weekend and in the lead-up to Windrush Day.

Paulette and Natalie went on *Good Morning Britain* and spoke openly about the impact the Windrush scandal was having on Paulette's mental health. Sadly, that was the last time the public saw Paulette alive, because, just a week or so after she did that interview, I got the news from her daughter that she had passed away in her sleep. I was absolutely devastated. Paulette was really struggling, and on the day we presented the petition she said, 'Patrick, I'm struggling with the compensation forms. It is just too much for me. I do not know what else to do.'

The system let her down big time, and the grief of her passing was felt by a lot of people, so I was determined that she had to have the special funeral that she deserved. It needed to reflect her life and the contribution she had made as a key campaigner in exposing the Windrush scandal.

When it comes to funerals, Caribbean communities know about good funerals, and we wanted Paulette to have one. Sadly, an unfortunate consequence of the scandal is that the family did not have the money to cover the funeral costs. I was so determined that Paulette Wilson was going to get the funeral she deserved that I started another GoFundMe campaign, and the public response was overwhelming. In less than a week we raised the funds for the funeral and had enough left over to install a blue plaque in her honour at the Wolverhampton Heritage Centre.

I remember going to Wolverhampton on the day of the funeral and worrying about the anger and grief that people were feeling because we all knew that Paulette's death was directly linked to the 'hostile environment' policy, and that it was yet another example of 'state violence and sufferation at the hands of Babylon'.[13] When I arrived at Paulette's home that morning it was very apparent that the family and the community were going to ignore the lockdown restrictions, because to adhere to the 30-person maximum would be an infringement on our ability to grief communally.

We all made sure that Paulette got the funeral she deserved. There was a horse and carriage procession that left her home in Heath Town and made its way to the New Testament Church of God less than half a mile away. People came from all around the country, including London, Manchester and Bristol, to show their respects to her and their solidarity around justice for the Windrush Generation. There must have been around 500 people following that procession, which was led by Nyabinghi drummers, and outside the church there was powerful rhythmic drumming, chanting and calls for justice. Some people were calling out her name, 'Paulette, Paulette, Paulette'. It was a very powerful occasion, and a fit and proper tribute celebrating Paulette's life.

Only 30 people could be inside the church, and I had the privilege to be one of them. I spoke about her life and read a poem as a tribute to the Windrush Generation. While the service in the church was going on, outside the drummers and the crowd continued creating a powerful spiritual connection to Paulette and the ancestors. Paulette was a Rastafarian by faith, and to acknowledge that as part of the ceremonial process, one of the two pastors officiating the service was a Rastafarian.

When the service finished, there was another procession as we made our way to the burial ground, which was about three miles away, and there were film crews everywhere. Those in the funeral procession were mourning her passing, celebrating her life, and continuing to raise awareness of the plight of those affected by the Windrush scandal.

One of the issues and tensions at the time was around the Covid-19 restrictions. However, the Council recognised that it would have been impossible to try to enforce it at that time, so over 200 people were at the burial plot, pouring libation, singing and dancing. All the male family members began putting the dirt into the grave, and then others joined in too, not just the men, but everyone was doing it as an expression of our collective mourning and showing our respects to Paulette. The displays of love, empathy and compassion were evident as we sang and rejoiced her life, and we found comfort in our grief as we were linked together by one common thread, Paulette. It was an intensely powerful funeral.

I have never been to a funeral like that before. It was special, because it was Paulette, and in my tribute to her, I said she was 'likkle but tallawah' – meaning 'small and impactful'. Months later,

I wrote an obituary in *The Guardian* so that others would know that she died a broken woman.[14]

Sadly, she is not the only one to be let down by the system or end up being broken and going on to meet the ancestors. What is even more disturbing is that it will continue to happen if the current government and future governments continue to implement the 'hostile environment' policy strategy and refuses to right the wrongs of the Windrush scandal that have caused so much cumulative trauma and grief to other human beings.

I, and others, grieve for Paulette. We grieve for those who died because of the scandal. Yet, in the midst of our grief, we are continuing to witness government failures to right their wrongs. We see the conveyor belt of families experiencing the deterioration of the mental health of their loved ones, and then having to cope with the aftermath of the passing of those loved ones. How are we, as a community, expected to heal from the community trauma when the needs of people impacted by the Windrush scandal are still not being met?

I am continuing to do my part, and am currently working with Associate Professor Rochelle Burgess of University College London (UCL) on a project called 'The Ties that Bind: Mapping the Intergenerational Mental Health Consequences of the Windrush Scandal'.[15] The project is using public art and research to capture evidence of the impact of the 'hostile environment' policy and the Windrush scandal on people's mental health, and the grief experienced by families after the passing of their loved ones.[16]

The Windrush scandal is an ongoing indictment of British society, and there is no justice, and no peace. This is not just about the individual trauma, grief and loss – this affects an entire community. The system has let down too many people and lives have been lost because of it, and without access to proper culturally appropriate mental health support services to help those going through what turns out to be one of the most traumatic periods of their lives, Black does crack!

Notes

1. https://acci.org.uk
2. www.santeproject.org.uk
3. Williams, W. (2018) *Windrush Lessons Learned Review: Independent Review by Wendy Williams*. London: Home Office. www.gov.uk/government/publications/windrush-lessons-learned-review
4. Williams, W. (2018) *Windrush Lessons Learned Review: Independent Review by Wendy Williams*. London: Home Office. www.gov.uk/government/publications/windrush-lessons-learned-review
5. Gentleman, A. (2022) 'Windrush scandal caused by "30 years of racist immigration laws" – report.' *The Guardian*, 29 May. www.theguardian.com/uk-news/2022/may/29/windrush-scandal-caused-by-30-years-of-racist-immigration-laws-report
6. BBC News (2019) 'Windrush: Migrant Dexter Bristol died from natural causes.' www.bbc.co.uk/news/uk-england-london-49966380
7. Gentleman, A. (2019) 'Windrush victim and campaigner Sarah O'Connor dies aged 57.' *The Guardian*, 19 September. www.theguardian.com/uk-news/2018/sep/19/windrush-victim-campaigner-sarah-oconnor-dies-aged-57
8. UK Visas and Immigration, Home Office and The Rt Hon. Sajid Javid MP (2019) 'Home Secretary launches Windrush Compensation Scheme.' New story, 3 April. www.gov.uk/government/news/home-secretary-launches-windrush-compensation-scheme
9. Nagesh, N. (2023) 'Windrush victims being failed by compensation scheme – report.' BBC News, 17 April. www.bbc.co.uk/news/uk-65264683
10. Gentleman, A. (2018) 'Woman nearly deported after 50 years in UK wins leave to remain.' *The Guardian*, 11 January. www.theguardian.com/uk-news/2018/jan/11/paulette-wilson-threatened-with-deportation-after-50-years-in-uk-leave-to-remain
11. Gentleman, A. (2020) 'Windrush scandal survivors deliver petition to No 10.' *The Guardian*, 19 June. www.theguardian.com/uk-news/2020/jun/19/windrush-scandal-survivors-deliver-petition-to-no-10
12. Williams, W. (2018) *Windrush Lessons Learned Review: Independent Review by Wendy Williams*. London: Home Office. www.gov.uk/government/publications/windrush-lessons-learned-review
13. Gentleman, A. (2020) 'Paulette Wilson: "A precious gem...broken by the UK government".' *The Guardian*, 24 July. www.theguardian.com/uk-news/2020/jul/24/paulette-wilson-a-precious-gem-broken-by-the-uk-government
14. Vernon, P. (2020) 'Paulette Wilson remembered by Patrick Vernon.' *The Guardian*, 14 December. www.theguardian.com/world/2020/dec/14/paulette-wilson-remembered-by-patrick-vernon

15. www.ucl.ac.uk/grand-challenges/case-studies/2021/sep/ties-bind-mapping-intergenerational-mental-health-consequences-windrush
16. UCL News (2022) 'Windrush scandal victims to speak up about mental health and trauma.' 20 April. www.ucl.ac.uk/news/2022/apr/windrush-scandal-victims-speak-about-mental-health-and-trauma

Memory

Amanda Inniss

I am the air surrounding you
I am that fresh morning dew
I am the rain that quenches women and men
I am pure love, pure energy, that will never ever end.

I am the wind that gently blows
I am the heat and the cold
I am the moon glow at midnight
I am in everything that feels right

I am the bird song at day break
I am with you when you wake

I am a life lived with no regrets
I am the colours of a vibrant sunset

I am a cool summers day
I am in each breath that you take
I am in everything you see
I am now, in your loving memory.

18 When Do We Grieve?

NusShen Ankhu (aka Davy Hay)

NusShen is an experienced managing director with a demonstrated history of over 35 years' experience working in the mental health field. He works in the third sector for Pattigift Therapy CIC, providing culturally congruent psychological therapies. These include psychotherapy, counselling, race and mental health training and healing circles. In his work he provides a community-focused safe space where African heritage people can explore their historical and contemporary challenges. NusShen is a recipient of the President's Award from the Association of Black Psychologists (USA) for 'advancing African-centred healing internationally'.

We Wear the Mask – Paul Laurence Dunbar[1]

We wear the mask that grins and lies,
It hides our cheeks and shades our eyes, –
This debt we pay to human guile;
With torn and bleeding hearts we smile,
And mouth with myriad subtleties.

Why should the world be over-wise,
In counting all our tears and sighs?
Nay, let them only see us, while
We wear the mask.

We smile, but, O great Christ, our cries
To thee from tortured souls arise.
We sing, but oh the clay is vile
Beneath our feet, and long the mile;
But let the world dream otherwise,
We wear the mask!

Grief...a feeling of great sadness, especially when someone dies

When the opportunity arose to write something about grief, bereavement and loss, I didn't go straight to thinking about my personal life. My spirit took me to thinking that grief for African heritage people has become a constant companion these past six hundred years or so. It is the very heavy overcoat that drapes around our shoulders, and it feels relentless.

The past few years has seen the conversation about grief become a theme – the onset of the Covid-19 pandemic and its disproportionate impact in the West on people of African heritage, bringing to the forefront the disparities in health, living conditions, labour and education.

The Covid-19 pandemic provided the latest statistics to join a disturbing pattern that illustrates all too clearly that despite the rhetoric over the years, this United Kingdom still doesn't value African heritage lives as much as their White counterparts.

Data published by the Office for National Statistics has shown that in England, the gap in life expectancy between the least and most deprived areas was 9.4 years for males and 7.4 years for females.[2] These differences in health outcomes are related to the overlapping, interrelated effects of long-term inequality and poverty, and African heritage people are disproportionately affected by these health inequalities.

We know that those in the African heritage community are

more likely to work in higher risk occupations and make up a disproportionate number of frontline staff and key workers, and were more likely to be impacted by the pandemic due to not being able to remote work. We see how our children were adversely affected by remote learning and school closings. Then we watched the latest presentation of trauma porn as George Floyd was being put to death in a street in the USA with his executioners showing no sense of uncertainty, without fear of retaliation, and clearly without any fear of being held accountable.

According to the *I Can't Breathe: Race, Death & British Policing* report,[3] here, in the UK, African heritage people have a propensity to find themselves dead in custody and in psychiatric hospitals in numbers greater than our percentage of the population. Families who are bereaved or who are grieving are regularly traumatised by an unjust system.

Then just for good measure let's add to the pot the consistently poor outcomes in mental health and maternal health, and the resulting associated traumas involved, and we have a recipe for a level of grief not often talked about let alone explored.

Excessive death in African heritage communities, whether from the pandemic, infant mortality or institutional violence, is one of the most disturbing consequences of institutional racism. This is not just about the loss of lives; the disaster is also in the grief and trauma these deaths bring to family, friends and community. In other words, we not only disproportionately face death; we must also deal with an almost overwhelming amount of grief and mourning.

This notion of grief as it relates to African heritage people is at odds with the grief model developed by Elisabeth Kubler-Ross,[4] employed in therapeutic settings for over 50 years, and often viewed as the 'gold standard'. Its stages of denial, anger, bargaining, depression and acceptance are in no way able to be a healing option for

'Black grief', which is continual and in many instances related to racial trauma.

Only two stages, anger and depression, have any meaning for African heritage people because, faced with consistent and constant incidents against us, we are always dealing with anger and depression. This is compounded by the paucity of available help, which leaves us unable to address the post-traumatic stress disorder (PTSD) and persistent trauma that is a relentless part of our lives.

Here are some common themes presented by African heritage people touched by grief.

Hopelessness

Hopelessness is a practice of acceptance whereby an African heritage person understands that loss is ever-present. No matter what safeguards they try to put in place, there will always be a sense of hopelessness in keeping themselves and their loved ones safe. In some cases, this 'living while Black' can contribute to the loss of life.

Self-reproach

Self-reproach can be a factor for African heritage people who have spent their lives trying to keep their loved ones safe in a social structure that places the safety of White people in higher regard. For African heritage people, self-reproach may be compounded by a belief that they were unsuccessful in keeping those close to them safe against the violence in all its forms of the social structure. When they hold a feeling of responsibility that doesn't belong to them, it belongs to the social structure they inhabit.

Taking action

Taking time to grieve and process loss is a privilege not readily available to African heritage people. The context around a death or serious trauma, social economic status and family relations may create a set of challenges that can complicate the process of dealing with the situation. Rest becomes a luxury and action becomes difficult for any communal support, particularly when unforeseen issues arise.

Fortitude

Often, African heritage people must find the resilience to endure with little outside support. After the immediate event has ended and things appear to return to some semblance of normality, the grieving process can deepen. The need to act makes it difficult for others to recognise the griever's vulnerabilities and cries for help. The perception of strength can be a barrier to aftercare even though the need for support increases. African heritage women, in particular, find themselves alone in their grief because they are socialised to be strong and stoic, to be the stereotypical 'strong Black woman'.

Persistence

For Black people, survival can be considered the new acceptance stage. To endure in a social structure weighted against them, they have no choice but to pull themselves together and continue to persevere. Factors such as economic challenges and living conditions will continue to impede the grieving process, but they must endure to progress. Consequently, sadness, anger and regret are a few emotions that may never totally diminish.

So what is to be done?

We need to find ways to support grief as a community, and our first port of call is to take a long look at the historical and contemporary experiences around death in African heritage communities, and be cognisant of the fact that the grief we experience is unique. Our grief has been compounded and exacerbated by racism and discrimination, beginning in enslavement and colonialism.

The psychological consequences that enslavement and colonialism have had on Africa and her people have yet to be fully addressed and understood. Africa lost millions of souls to the slave trade. This human derailment was experienced at the personal level as psychic terror and physical torture.[5] The colonisation of continental Africa resulted in similar psychological terror and torture. Despite what many outside the Black community and some within may suggest, the impact of over 600 years of terror did not end with the abolition of enslavement or the number of African nations becoming independent in the 1960s.

A question I often pose is, when did we heal from this? Because many of us act as if we have healed, and that the past is past and has no bearing on the present. This historical terrorism is compounded by ongoing injustices, whether it be violent, as in Buffalo, NY, where a gunman killed ten people in a racist attack,[6] or 'Child Q', the Black school girl who was strip-searched by the police in London,[7] or the insidiousness of microaggressions, and since African heritage families experience loss more than any other racial group,[8] any new bereavement can trigger painful memories and further compound loss and grief.

We have to be prepared to acknowledge the traumas we have experienced, both historical and contemporary, for they are connected.

A next step is the centring of Black grief. We are used to a narrow definition of grief that doesn't account for more collective loss. What are the customs, beliefs and rituals we have that can be utilised in the service of managing grief? Many may not been transmitted generationally or are not considered sophisticated enough.

Pattigift Therapy,[9] the organisation I work for, provides several programmes underpinned by African-centred psychology.[10] The Association of Black Psychologists adopted the following definition of African-centred psychology to guide theory, research, practice and action: 'Black/African Centred psychology is a dynamic manifestation of unifying African principles, values, and traditions that are reflected within broader Pan-African or transcultural communities'.[11]

African-centred psychology, as a system of thought and action, examines the processes that allow for the illumination and liberation of the Spirit. Relying on the principles of harmony within the universe as a natural order of existence, African-centred psychology recognises: the Spirit that permeates everything, that is, the notion that everything in the universe is interconnected; the value that the collective is the most salient element of existence; and the idea that communal self-knowledge is the key to mental health. This suggests that people of African heritage share certain characteristics based on similar cultural experiences that include, but are not limited to: (1) supremacy of community; (2) a high level of spirituality and ethical concern; (3) harmony with nature; and (4) believing in the interrelatedness and interconnectedness of all things in the universe.[12]

We often consider our sojourn through enslavement and colonialism as something to be ashamed of, but if we take a step back, we can see that we were not meant to survive and yet here we are, our very presence testimony to our resilience and our spirituality. We have a deep cultural well with which to draw on.

We should be considering ways of bringing spiritual traditions within our communities to work in conjunction with therapy organisations to co-produce culturally affirming programmes to promote healing. These should be group- or community-focused rather than individual, in keeping with our cultural orientations.

We need to remember and rekindle our ways of knowing in relation to how we grieve and how we deal with bereavement and loss. Utilising our traditional ways of dealing with grief helps to ground us; it helps to remind us of who we are. If you take stock and look at most rituals we practice when dealing with grief and loss, we never stopped being African. We may adapt it, give it different names, add different identities, even run from describing it as African, but at its core ask yourself where these practices come from. Where you're born and where you're from is not always the same thing. We must reclaim the momentum of memory.

We already have the tools we need to provide support and healing to our communities; we just need to decolonise ourselves from fear-based ways of knowing and living.

The poem at the beginning of this chapter speaks to the way we have become socialised to present a face to the world that hides the pain we feel so as not to make others feel discomfort. It was a survival tactic that was necessary in times gone by. But it's time now to put away the mask and be at peace with expressing our grief. To speak our truth to the world.

Ankh udja seneb [Wishing you life, prosperity and health].

Notes

1. Dunbar, P.L. (1913) 'We Wear the Mask.' In *The Complete Poems of Paul Laurence Dunbar*. New York: Dodd, Mead & Co.

2. ONS (Office for National Statistics) (2018) 'Suicides in the UK: 2017 registrations.' www.ons.gov.uk/peoplepopulationandcommunity/birthsdeathsandmarriages/deaths/bulletins/suicidesintheunitedkingdom/2017registrations

3. INQUEST (2023) *I Can't Breathe: Race, Death & British Policing*. Full report. London: INQUEST. www.inquest.org.uk/i-cant-breathe-race-death-british-policing

4. Kübler-Ross, E. (1973) *On Death and Dying*. London: Routledge.

5. Nobles. W.W. (2013) 'Shattered consciousness, fractured identity: Black psychology and the restoration of the African psyche.' *Journal of Black Psychology 39*, 3, 232–242. https://doi.org/10.1177/0095798413478075

6. BBC News (2022) 'Buffalo shooting: Ten dead in racially motivated attack at New York state store.' 15 May. www.bbc.co.uk/news/world-us-canada-61452958

7. BBC News (2022) 'Child Q: Strip-search Met Police officers facing gross misconduct case.' 14 June. www.bbc.co.uk/news/uk-england-london-61796798

8. Commission on Race and Ethnic Disparities (2021) *The Report of the Commission on Race and Ethnic Disparities*. London: The Stationery Office. www.gov.uk/government/publications/the-report-of-the-commission-on-race-and-ethnic-disparities

9. www.pattigifttherapy.com

10. Parham, T. A., White, J.L. and Ajamu, A. (1999) *The Psychology of Blacks: African-Centered Perspective*. Upper Saddle River, NJ: Prentice Hall.
11. Myers, L.J. and Speight, S.L. (2010) 'Reframing mental health and psychological well-being among persons of African descent: Africana/Black psychology meeting the challenges of fractured social and cultural realities.' *The Journal of Pan African Studies 3*, 8, 66–82. www.jpanafrican.org/docs/vol3no8/3.8ReframingMentalcorrection.pdf
12. Myers, L.J. (1988 [1992]) *Understanding an Afrocentric World View: Introduction to an Optimal Psychology*. Dubuque, IA: Kendall/Hunt.

19 Not All Grief is the Same: A Funeral Celebrant's Perspective

Debi Lewinson Roberts

Debi works with the bereaved (or the deceased before they transition) to put together person-centred funeral ceremonies and memorials to give fitting and inclusive farewells. She uses her working knowledge of culture, tradition, religion and spirituality and her experiential knowledge of African Caribbean funeral practices to work through complex sets of emotions in a meaningful way to devise ceremonies across a wide range of beliefs and backgrounds. In addition, Debi offers a virtual space to facilitate 'Loss Cafés' for the Black African diaspora to discuss racial and culturally sensitive topics related to death, dying, bereavement and grieving. Debi also has a background in education, training and development, not-for-profit management and project management.

We all grieve differently, and of all the mental health challenges facing people, many thousands are enduring that grief often silently and alone. For some people it's a process, with a beginning, a middle and thankfully, an end. For others, it's a lifelong condition – a new state of being following the death of a loved one.

Grief is not just individual; it's also cultural.

Paul McLean became a funeral director when he experienced first hand the double suicide of his sister and niece, which was followed by an upsetting lack of understanding of the needs of African diaspora people in an overwhelmingly White profession.

I know a bit about grief too. I am an independent celebrant who has suffered bereavement. I set up Serenity Gardens[1] offering person-centred funeral ceremonies and memorials that are based on the culture, tradition, religion or spirituality of the client. I also set up the Loss Café. The Café is sometimes virtual, sometimes a real-world place of refuge where Black people can share their grief and provide mutual support.

I often work with Paul on the most challenging funerals, especially in the case of violent deaths and including suicide, bringing comfort in the worst of circumstances.

When carrying out funerals there are people who want a little bit of religion while others want none at all, and as I work from a person-centred perspective, I am happy to go with whatever feels right for them.

My father was a minister, so I was raised to comfort the bereaved, support the community and attend funerals from childhood. As an independent celebrant I work for the family and ensure that everything I do is about them, rather than the funeral process itself taking over and pushing them in directions they don't want to go. Families often choose to work with me rather than a minister because of my flexible approach and because I don't conform to the structures of any specific faith. Instead, I design services to complement the wishes and beliefs of the families.

If someone doesn't want the rigidity of a humanist celebrant or a religious minister, that's when they will consider the services of an independent celebrant. I usually work alone, but I have also served alongside religious leaders from different faiths. I have led a service for a family who were Methodists from South Africa, but who also had Hindu traditions, so I created a blended funeral by inviting a Hindu priest who conducted the traditional rites ceremony and the Methodist minister spoke. The various traditions and religions were woven together – the result was what the family wanted and they were very pleased.

Being a good celebrant is also about being a good storyteller. The funeral is where you tell the story of someone's life so I always talk to family members in detail about the person who has died so I can write a eulogy that's fitting. Whether I read it myself or write it for a relative to read from their own personal perspective, it is a huge responsibility to get it right.

Grief and guilt entwined

For Paul and his wife Sharon, who together run Integrity Funeral Care in London, attention to detail is extremely important.

People need funerals to go smoothly as part of that grieving process. One of the reasons that Paul and Sharon founded the business in the first place was the lack of understanding of the specific cultural needs of Black people. We hold what's called Nine Night celebrations, a traditional get-together, usually before the funeral takes place, where everyone can celebrate the life that has ended.

Our community is used to funerals that can take several hours in church and then a couple more hours by the graveside, with songs and poems and speeches. It can be so upsetting if a funeral director or a minister doesn't understand the importance of those traditions. It's not that they're better or worse than anyone else's way of doing things, but it's how people need to express themselves and to hopefully begin a process of healing. Attention to detail is everything. Paul and I know from personal experience how grief can be compounded if a funeral doesn't feel exactly right. When things aren't as they should be, families can feel guilty that they've let down the loved one who's passed.

It's been widely reported how the pandemic and lockdowns disrupted so many funerals. When everything was in crisis, many important traditional elements got lost, such as washing, dressing and viewing the body, Nine Night celebrations and the mourners coming together over food. Everything became so much harder, which amplified the grief people felt.

Family and friends often couldn't be at the graveside, and if they were, they couldn't help fill the grave because they weren't allowed to touch any of the tools. Some of the White funeral directors I worked with became a lot less accommodating, even in terms of explaining to families what was and wasn't possible.

I have always tried to make sure the family had all the necessary information in advance because it was just awful when, on the day of the funeral, the funeral directors would just almost shrug their shoulders at the graveside and say, 'Oh, yeah, sorry; can't do that'.

What's left when all the mourners have gone?

I became a Death Café facilitator in 2017. I didn't know of any other Black people running one, and I wanted the space to be multi-cultural, as all the cafés I visited weren't very diverse and I didn't feel particularly welcome. I wanted to celebrate different types of people, so when lockdown came, I thought it was an opportunity to go online and start a Loss Café for people from the African diaspora. Now that it's virtual we've got people coming from the African continent, from the USA, Canada and the Caribbean, as well as the UK.

The Loss Café is a safe platform where people can talk about what they're going through. Individuals share as much as they want, or they just listen. People are encouraged to share because the more they do, the more they get out of it. Others offer support by saying for example, 'When my mum died, this is how I dealt with it.' Or 'When my husband was in the hospital and the doctors weren't listening to me, this is what I did...' Or 'This is how I spoke to my children about my diagnosis.' People talk about their fears, but they also talk about their challenges.

I also helped in the setting up of a grief support group run by Black men for Black men. I remember Paul saying that that men don't always want to talk in front of women, especially because some of the conversations that they deal with are what they see as specifically male problems, whether it's to do with relationships, physical or mental health or emotions.

One of the main reasons that Paul works with me is because we both recognise that in our culture, from the moment of loss to the funeral and beyond, it is different from the British norm. He wants the process to be seamless for the families he works with, so he will hand over his delicate clients to someone like me to manage the day itself, whether it be the eulogy or other elements.

We've seen and experienced how it helps people when they feel that their culture, their understanding, their needs as Black people are fully met without reservation. We even have families who didn't need my services for the funeral, but who Paul has put me in touch with afterwards, for that post-funeral care.

Grieving is different for everyone. People may live with their grief forever, as it's a process without time limits. That we are there for them, to support them in their time of need, is what really matters.

Notes

1.   https://facfo.org/serenity-gardens

20 Community Goodwill in Times of Grief: #UGiveHope

Brian Quavar

Brian is London born, of Jamaican and Trinidadian parentage. His passion is photography, capturing people, spaces and events that reflect the beauty of the African and Caribbean diaspora through his eyes. He finds peace and solace and joy and motivation in photography, which helps him to keep the memory of his loved ones alive. He is an Underground train driver and a community advocate.

Brian advocates for open and frank conversations about health and wellbeing in the Black community, and as a recent prostate cancer survivor he speaks openly about his journey. He talks about the fears, the highs, the lows and the uncomfortable issues that people often shy away from, with the hope that it will encourage others to be mindful of their own health and wellbeing.

It is early April 2020 and England is on lockdown. I had returned from the Trinidad and Tobago Carnival just a few weeks earlier, and on the flight back I was already planning for Carnival 2023 and looking forward to my next overseas trip. Instead, there was a total lockdown!

Work and essential trips only, the government mandated, as the daily news was flooded with reports of rising Covid-19 deaths and hospitalisations.

Loneliness and isolation were residing side by side with fear and trepidation and heavy doses of online misinformation and conspiracy theories.

Voices in the Black community were crying out for help. Our People are dying! Our People are struggling! Young people are scared; their anxiety is rising. Something needs to be done.

Our community needed uplifting, people needed to be able to hold on to hope, and when my colleague Dr Yansie Rolston suggested that we host an online entertainment event on the communications platform Zoom, I was all up for the idea. We had both participated in international concerts and events before – she as an organiser and performer, and I as a photographer – so our contact lists came in handy. The following week #UGiveHope Fridays was born.

Hosting, performing and viewing live entertainment via Zoom was a first for us, and during this period Zoom was also learning how to host live entertainment and school lessons on its platform, so we were learning alongside them... We just knew that we had to do something to bring some joy back into the lives of people from the Black community, and give them a space where they could be distracted from the seriousness of what was happening as they were going about their daily lives under a cloud of fear and uncertainty.

Lockdown lasted just under two years, and by the end of it #UGiveHope had showcased over one hundred artistes and performers of the African and Caribbean diaspora from 31 countries across the globe. They all gave their time for free, spreading joy and giving hope to anyone who logged on. Some Fridays there were only 21 people online; other times there were around 900 of us, all spending time together, singing, dancing, laughing, or just looking on and enjoying the entertainment.

It was a distraction (even if it was only for a few hours) from the turmoil of grief and bereavement that was happening across the world. All of us were coping with the loss of loved ones, colleagues, friends and neighbours. No one was immune to the grief, but we all logged on to #UGiveHope to find comfort in community. Whether it was actual loss due to death, estrangement, the impact of isolation or the absence of physical contact with loved ones, friends or colleagues, we were all grieving.

As the weeks turned into months, #UGiveHope became its own community within a community. A family unit was formed, but it was a family with a difference. There was a core group who would log on every week without fail – 'the regulars' – and we shared our ups and downs, our pain and sorrows, our joys and endless laughter. Most of us had never met in person, but we cried together, sharing some of the most intimate parts of our lives, and long-lasting friendships and romantic relationships were formed all because the space was sacred, comforting and healing.

The family

#UGiveHope depended on the community spirit of goodwill. There was no funding to pay artistes, yet they turned up and performed from their heart, determined to spread messages of joy, and they gave hope to all who tuned in.

We saw a constant flow of WhatsApp messages about the passing of a friend or relation, news reports highlighting the disproportionate number of deaths in the Black community, email links to GoFundMe pages asking for help to save a community group at risk of closure, and phone calls saying that people were struggling with their mental health. Amid all that, the global African and Caribbean diaspora continued to come together – the audience, artistes and hosts coming together to find solace and comfort in the space.

It was not all smooth-sailing, though. Racists tried to disrupt the vibe with 'Zoom bombings', which happened at our biggest session, when at its peak well over 1000 had joined online. Half an hour into the performances, the vile racist comments started with a vengeance, and as fast as we blocked one, another would pop up. When the racism didn't stop the show, they took over the screen with hardcore porn imagery. It was a challenge, but the community is resilient and refused to let the racist disruptors win. The show had to go on!

Some of the audience acted as lookouts for the disrupters, throwing them off Zoom as soon as they posted their vile racist comments. I do often wonder what goes on in the mind of another human being that drives them to be so inhumane, especially at a time when the world was in such utter turmoil.

At the end of that night, I cried for several minutes with relief. I was alone at home, with no one there to offer me comfort, so I sat and let the tears cascade down my face. Then suddenly a feeling of pride washed over me. I felt proud knowing that the racists hadn't stolen our joy, and despite #UGiveHope being so new, we had already become a fantastic community. The strength of the #UGiveHope family allowed us to survive the torrent of abuse. We were a family who supported each other.

Not long after that incident one of the performers from Cameroon lost her mother. She logged on and performed through her tears and we all sang along with her, wept with her and grieved with her – we were her #UGiveHope family.

When one of the Haitian artistes reached out to say that her internet was not working, her #UGiveHope family provided her with a mobile data card. We were all a family that cared for each other. We signposted performers and guests to mental health services, helped with writing CVs, catered lunches for those in need and attended virtual birthday get-togethers. One person described it as 'our church'. Another said it was a 'home away from home even, though I was at home'. Another described it as 'my personal at-home house party'. To this day the #UGiveHope family continues to be united.

One thing I have discovered in this journey is that there are many facets to grief, loss and bereavement, and that it is not just about grieving the loss of a loved one, friend, family member or pet. The loss of freedom of movement, the isolation and lack of physical contact affected me. I was suddenly unable to visit my mother who lived in New York when prior to the pandemic I would pay her an annual surprise visit, sometimes more than once per year. Travel restrictions stopped those visits and those were very tough times for both my mother and me. Mum looked forward to those visits, and constantly told me how much she was grieving the distance between us.

My dad had transitioned to the ancestral realm in 2002 and mum has been grieving for him since then. They had been together for over 40 years, and when he passed, her world stood still. She found the emptiness overwhelming, and her grief escalated on what would have been special days that she shared with dad – wedding anniversaries, birthdays and Christmases. Hearing her crying on those days was gut-wrenching because I knew that nothing could console her.

Mum and I spoke regularly, and when she was finally persuaded to get a smartphone, we would video call while I was out taking long walks along the river, showing her the sights and sounds along the way. The pandemic restrictions meant that those walks no longer happened. She missed the virtual tours, and I missed taking her on them.

Mum's sparkle faded with time. I sensed the escalation of her grief and the depression that was beginning to set in as time went on, but I could not help her, and that caused my own feelings of loss, isolation and grief to increase. I was no longer able to give her the surprise visits that she looked forward to; I could not see her in her home environment to be sure that she had the things she needed or to do those little DIY jobs that she saved for when I visited. I, too, was battling depression, and thankfully #UGiveHope gave me some relief, something to occupy my mind every week.

When the travel restrictions were eased, I was overjoyed, but mum was unvaccinated, and because we both had underlying health conditions, we decided that I should not risk travelling abroad. Then, in December 2021, we stopped the online #UGive-Hope Fridays because socialising in person became more desirable, even though there was still a lot of anxiety about venturing out to crowded places. Covid-19 was still real. Even though we didn't meet online every Friday, the #UGiveHope family stayed connected, communicating regularly. We missed the regular Friday evening get-together, and there was a real feeling of loss.

Time moved on and life was beginning to return to some semblance of normality. I started videoing mum again as I went on my walks, and she would enjoy seeing the ducks on the river and the flowers on the paths, but she wasn't too keen on the aeroplane noises in the background, and I don't blame her.

Then, towards the end of 2021, her health deteriorated dramatically. She had a dry cough, shortness of breath, no taste, loss of energy – some of the classic Covid-19 symptoms – but she was adamant she didn't want to get tested. To say that the family were concerned is an understatement. As time went on, she got weaker, and the heartache of helplessness for all who loved her increased, but mum was used to being a proud, independent woman, and was not going to give up that independence.

The harshness of winter was gripping New York, and my concern was growing with each passing day, but she tried to reassure me that she was beginning to feel better. I knew that the weather, the isolation, the depression and the complications of her health were all taking their toll on her, so I decided that I would visit her as soon as it was possible to do so.

My phone rang just before midnight on 3rd February 2022 – exactly 20 years to the day I got the call from mum telling me that dad had passed. The voice on the other end of the phone said that mum had collapsed in the bathroom and had passed.

Suddenly it felt as though someone had pressed a pause button. Everything became a blur; time stood still, except for the pounding in my heart. Mum and I had spoken the day before. She told me to take care of myself and that she'd be okay. Just a few hours before she passed one of her grandchildren let her know that she was making plans to visit her from Ghana soon, but mum told her not to come. Did mum have a premonition?

My parents' love for each other was so strong to the very end that mum passed on the anniversary of dad's passing. I called my partner and told her that 'dad came to get his wife'.

What followed was sadness, anger, frustration, guilt and sorrow. Tears flowed, voices raised and grief took a hold of me. The grief gripped me like a vice, and at times it felt like it just would not let go. My heart hurt, my body ached, my brain sometimes went numb. I cried, I wept, I sobbed, I laughed.

There were practical things that needed to be done so I tried not to give in to the emotions, at least not just yet. But grief and loss do not work with logic, and I would be on the phone making funeral arrangements when suddenly I would remember something really humorous that she had said, and I would have to stifle a laugh. Seconds later the reality that she would no longer be accompanying me virtually on the walks by the river kicked in and I would sob uncontrollably.

I miss my dad and I miss my mum, and now, more than ever, I appreciate the love and support I get from the #UGiveHope family.

Notes

1. Thomson, L. (2023) 'Black men are more likely to get prostate cancer. We need to talk about it.' *Metro*, 14 October. https://metro.co.uk/2023/10/14/black-men-more-likely-to-get-prostate-cancer-we-need-to-discuss-it-19627145

21 Coming Together in Hope: A Service of Reflection

Reverend Cassius Francis

Cassius is a minister with the Wesleyan Holiness Church, and church trainer and resourcer with Loss and HOPE,[1] a Christian coalition project of the UK's bereavement signposting and information website, AtaLoss.[2] He also works as a chaplain at Birmingham Women's and Children's Hospital. Cassius realised that he had to do more work to understand how to support bereaved families after his first funeral for an 11-year-old boy and the deaths of two close friends. He also understood the need to strengthen his own mental health. Cassius is a proud Brummie, a Spurs supporter, and has been married to Vanessa for 25 years.

'Coming Together in Hope: A Service of Reflection for Black Communities affected by Covid-19 Pandemic' was held on Wednesday 23rd March 2022 at the New Life Wesleyan Church in Birmingham as part of the National Day of Reflection coordinated by the bereavement charity Marie Curie to mark the first day of our national lockdown in 2020.

It was important that we could meet in person for this service, as churches had been closed for much of the pandemic, but this was a hybrid service so people could also watch a live broadcast online. It was a Christian service to which everyone was invited.

One important part of it was playing a song by the London Community Gospel Choir (LCGC) called 'Sun in the Rain' and a roll call of deceased names from Black communities affected and children and/or young people in the planning and/or delivery of the service.

During the pandemic three of our ministers had died and our churches were obviously supporting grieving families in their congregations and communities. Alongside all of this was a tangible awareness of the disproportionate impact of Covid-19 on Black communities, not just nationally, but also globally. The service also reflected on the journey over the last two years and what practitioners supporting bereaved Black families could learn from the process.

One of our churches had been supporting a family whose matriarch had died in February 2020. She had been a member of the Wesleyan Holiness Church for over 50 years, so she was also a matriarch in the church. At that point, for most of us Covid-19 was being treated as more of a rumour than anything to be concerned about. For this family the plans for a large funeral, very common in the African Caribbean community, were thrown into chaos by the lockdown. Any plans for hundreds of mourners, multiple people taking part in the service and a reception with people to enjoy food, share stories, reminisce, show support and bring comfort were reduced to the need for a restriction of 12 people to attend the funeral.

The rules on restricted numbers to attend funeral gatherings impacted families up and down the country, but were particularly keenly felt by families in our Black communities. That was a key reason for wanting to put on the service of reflection in March 2022 – in recognition of the fact that there were many, many Black families who had not been able to have the funeral for their loved one that they would have wanted. There was a weighty sense of personal responsibility in recognising the grief that people had been holding could result in a huge outpouring of emotion on the day, so counsellors were in place to provide support.

While I had a really strong sense that the service was the right thing to do, I was faced with my own personal challenges. I was grieving the death of my nan in July 2021. Then, on the night of Tuesday 2nd November 2021, my dad was admitted to hospital after contracting Covid-19. It was an extremely traumatic time, coming so soon after my nan's death earlier in the year, but also because my dad is diabetic, and we knew that he was already in a high risk group with Covid-19.

In hindsight I can see how focusing on the planning for the service helped me to maintain a wider sense of perspective, but this backdrop meant juggling daily communication to the hospital with my brother and sister, supporting my mom, keeping the wider family and church updated and trying to continue the day jobs – as a Christian minister I was engaged in supporting other families, and no doubt similar stories have been replicated thousands of times up and down the country.

I am grateful to God for keeping me and my family through that time. There were lots of prayers and lots of tears, and on three occasions my dad had to be resuscitated. I am grateful to my church family and wider family for their consistent support, and to the NHS for the fact that we live in a country with free healthcare. However, what surprised me was just how debilitating that time was. It felt as if dad was in prison, as we couldn't see him. We relied on calls to the hospital to check on how dad was, which wasn't great. Sometimes the communication came across as inconsistent.

I struggled with the guilt of wondering whether we would see my dad alive again. I was exhausted, and I was amazed as I saw how as a large family everyone was involved in trying to support dad through this at a distance. I regularly wondered about how people coped without those extended networks if they were in a similar situation. In Chimamanda Ngozi Adichie's book *Notes on Grief*, she writes about the experience of losing both her father and her mother during the course of the pandemic. I just can't imagine the sense of loss.

It was against this personal backdrop that the service of re-flection was planned.[3] I have included some of the details of the service here.

- Prelude: Reflections Worship by Seth Pinnock and A New Thing. Music and singing are critical aspects to unite Black communities through funeral rituals, so it was important to start the service this way, and to have young people leading in this component.

- Song: 'Sun in the Rain' by the London Community Gospel Choir (LCGC). The song was gifted by LCGC to support the Majonzi Fund,[4] so using it was a way of raising awareness about the fund, and encouraging people to find out more if they had not heard about it.

- Welcome and Opening Prayer by Reverend Ruth Lowe, Wes-leyan Holiness Church. The leader of the Wesleyan church, Reverend Ruth Lowe, a Black female minister, acted as a host for the service, welcoming people, providing the context to this service of lament and the important role she and the church played supporting bereaved families throughout the pandemic across the country.

- Why this Gathering: Professor Patrick Vernon OBE, Majonzi Fund. Patrick shared his personal experiences of bereave-ment during the pandemic. He also spoke about the broader community concerns of not being able to gather together to support each other, not being able to have the Nine Night traditional funeral rituals that the community was used to having, and not being allowed to say goodbye to loved ones in the traditional way. He poignantly said, 'People have suffered silently in pain...' But he encouraged those at the service and watching online to have hope as well as the importance of having salvation. 'Why are Black, South Asian and Filipino communities disproportionately reflected in the Covid-19 death rates?' he asked, rhetorically.

- Scripture reading, Psalm 46: 1–11 'God's Defence of His City and People'. A pre-recorded compilation of 'selfie' videos coordinated by Richard Reddie from Churches Together in Britain and Ireland,[5] an ecumenical entity supporting and encouraging churches from a wide range of traditions to work together in unity. The impact of people reading in different languages and with different accents, and from different denominational backgrounds and different ages, was significant, and demonstrated the global and cross-generational impact of the pandemic.

- Song: 'Poor Wayfaring Stranger (Traditional)' by Black Voices. Black Voices, which was formed in 1987 by its music director Carol Pemberton MBE, has gained a reputation as Europe's finest female a cappella quintet. Their home, Grosvenor Road Studios, is Birmingham's oldest recording studio, and Black Voices has touched the world; the audience was blessed to hear this special performance live.

I Am a Poor Wayfaring Stranger

[Verse 1]
I am a poor, wayfaring stranger
While travelling through this world of woe.
But there's no sickness, toil nor danger
In that bright land to which I go.

[Chorus]
I'm going there to see my mother
I'm going there no more to roam
I'm only going over Jordan
And I'm only going over home

[Verse 2]
I know dark clouds may hover o'er me
I know that my way will be rough and steep
But golden fields, lie on before me
In that bright land, where we'll never sleep

[Chorus]
I'm going there to see my brother
I'm going there no more to roam
I'm only going over Jordan
I'm only going over home

[Scat]

[Chorus]
I'm going there to see my Saviour
I'm going there, no more to roam
I'm only going over Jordan
I'm only going over home.

- Prayers of Reflection by Janet Smith, Wolverhampton Black Business Network and JS Associates and Carol Jacobs, Evangelical Alliance: Janet prayed about the impact on the business community, and Black businesses in particular, and spoke of the importance of sustaining dreams during difficult times. The audience was asked to remember the healthcare workers and first responders, and to pray for strength and renewing.

  The lights in the church were dimmed and candles were lit at this point as a symbolic recognition of those who had died. Carol then read Psalm 23 'The Lord is My Shepherd...', which is often read at funeral services. She prayed about the injustices that Black communities have continued to face throughout the pandemic, and for the strength to forgive those who had wronged the community. Carol also referenced Psalm 34: 18, 'The Lord Is Close to the Broken-Hearted...', and prayed for healing and a sense of closure for those who had lost loved ones.

Young people were key in this service, and Dawn Thomas transfixed the audience with her poem and recital, which captured the mixture of emotions both throughout the pandemic, and also for the evening.

Poem by Dawn Thomas

I've been waiting for this moment
Because it felt like time stood still
We were behind closed doors enduring loss and grief
Without the usual to console
We lost people, jobs, peace, joy, moments and time
And at times hope was hard to keep alive
Because we was thrusted into moments where all we could see present
in life was loss

A Society led full of fear and all we could hear was that planted fear
So, I turned my news notifications off
But what couldn't be turned off was the reality of loss
And in the midst of this global pandemic my ethnicity was still a global
pandemic
Racial inequality became a priority
We was fighting for our lives, but not just because of Covid
But now because the colour of my skin continued to be an issue in this
modern 21st century society

All we could feel was loss and pain
But we still had to fight to keep our hope alive again and again
Moments of reminiscing on their memories brought comfort and a
smile

But broken hearts still remain
Hurt and tears did not refrain
And nearly two years later many of us are still in pain
And are traumatised from this pandemic that has taken place

And now in this moment of reflection I'm propelled to reflect on my
anchor
Because in the moments of the feelings of defeat
There was an anchor that continued to hold you and me though the
storms of life
Your anchor remained through it all
Even when the storms were raging, you were never ignored
God saw it all
And as the storm begins to fade
There are still pieces that need to be put back together again
It's okay to be broken
We have a potter, the moulder of clay
And when broken and in pieces He does not refuse you
But He loves you
He holds you
He stays close to you
And He mends you

He saw you in the midst of loss
He saw you when you were at a loss for words
He saw you every day behind closed doors
He saw you when you held back the tears because you were trying to be
strong He saw you drop your anchor in the midst of the storm
Because you were holding on to the Word of the Lord

This is the God who sees and He held you through it all
So even as this storm fades may your anchors remain in the One who
is able to save And the residue of the brokenness left after the storm

COMING TOGETHER IN HOPE

Let those pieces be moulded and formed by the Father
The God who sees all
And remember,
The Lord is close to the broken-hearted
And His love will never ever be departed.

- Talking Drums by Nicky Reid and roll call of names by Reverend Cassius Francis. I led the roll call of names of community individuals who had died during the past two years, and the invitation was extended to the audience to also call out a name or to sit in quiet contemplation. I started the roll call with my nan's name, Inez Pauline Pemberton, who had died in July 2021. I trembled as I held the microphone for others sharing the names of their loved ones who had died over the last year, with one person calling out the names of four family members. Many commented afterwards that they were so overcome with emotion that it was impossible for them to say the name of the loved one who had died.
- Homily: 'Coming Together in Hope' by Bishop Mike, Churches Together in England. Bishop Mike said that despite all that had happened it was still possible to sing of the goodness of the Lord such as Psalm 46, which is a song that starts in a place of disorientation. He reminded the audience that in February 2022 the UK was hit by three storms – Dudley, Eunice and Franklin – and that the pandemic and the Windrush scandal were storms that Black communities have had to contend with, and the storm of war in Ukraine, which was exacerbating the cost-of-living crisis and hitting the poorest hardest, was also disproportionately impacting Black communities.
- Act of Remembrance (libation, the pouring of water) by Reverend Dr Joe Aldred and Song: 'Precious Memories' from Diane Wallace and Melvin Hare of Wesleyan Holiness Church. Diane, accompanied by Melvin on piano, gave a moving

rendition of 'Precious Memories', which is well known in Black Majority Churches and often sung at funeral services. Reverend Dr Joe gave context to the significance of the bay tree plant that he was going to water, which has medicinal qualities well known in Black Caribbean communities. He then read the following:

The Psalmist says, 'There is a river whose streams make glad the city of God, the holy place where the Most High dwells. He leads me besides still waters, He restores my soul.' Our African ancestors and religious communities around the world recognise water as a life-giving source, the use of which can remind us that in the midst of death there is life. So corporately we call to mind all those we've lost during this Covid pandemic, and each of us recall those who were nearest and dearest to us. We remember them with precious memories in the name of the Father (pouring water), in the name of the Son (pouring water), and in the name of the Holy Spirit (pouring water). Amen.

• Closing: The Lord's Prayer and Blessing by Reverend Ruth Lowe. The unison of the Lord's Prayer was symbolic. The prayers were led by Reverend Ruth Lowe as an important signal of her leadership of the church through this crisis. An invitation was extended to anyone wanting to speak with counsellors or to be referred to organisations listed in the order of service for further information and support afterwards.

My hope

While I am still coming to terms with the death of my nan, I find comfort knowing that at the time of her funeral (27th August 2021), attendance numbers were not restricted because many have not had that opportunity. While my dad had spent months in hospital, we were able to welcome him home, even though it felt as if my brother and I were engaged in a prison break to get him out (that is a whole other story) – he is home! Even with his health complications, he is home! Many have not been able to welcome their loved ones home.

I am comforted that I have been able to write a piece like this because there are many others with their own stories to tell for whom the grief is still too raw to express, or they just do not have the opportunity to share.

My hope is that this piece shows what can be done when you engage with heart matters because, as a Christian minister, I feel that the service of reflection provided a forum of healing for many people in Black communities, and demonstrated the important role that the church and faith have in helping people to process their grief.

I also hope that it inspires others to think about what they can do on an individual level to help meet the needs of their community. This is not a party political broadcast, but more of a call to promote more local 'activism', although I am not ignorant of my privileged position as a Christian minister and the networks that I had access to through this process.

I would like the government, political parties of all colours and decision-makers to truly understand the importance of authentic engagement. Black communities are not hard to reach! However, engagement needs to be authentic and transparent if injustices and inequalities are going to be addressed.

Notes

1. www.lossandhope.org
2. www.ataloss.org
3. The service can be viewed at www.youtube.com/watch?v=ZM61sMz_T_E
4. www.majonzi-fund.com
5. https://ctbi.org.uk

Hope Renewed

Amanda Inniss

As I raise my head to welcome a new day
I stand, both feet grounded to absorb healing rays
Everything I thought I knew, now has changed
I wondered if I would ever survive
Through the long days of endless nights
To reach this moment, to gradually feel sunlight
New colours fill my tear-stained view
For now, I look beyond me and you
The future once barren, once bleak,
Forms new summits and new peaks

I no longer cry, I no longer weep,
For I am stronger, I am grateful
And I am living with hope renewed
For this moment in my life, I carry on without you.

Useful Organisations and Resources

ACCI (African Caribbean Community Initiative), at the forefront of supportive services for individuals affected by mental ill health as well as continuing to raise awareness within the local community: https://acci.org.uk

AFT (Association for Family Therapy) is working to benefit the public by promoting effective Family and Systemic Psychotherapy services and high standards of professional training and practice: www.aft.org.uk

Ancestral Voices, an educational initiative documenting and disseminating research-based knowledge about African cosmologies and spiritual philosophies: https://ancestralvoices.co.uk

AtaLoss, helping bereaved people to find support and wellbeing: www.ataloss.org

Balanced Wheel exists to simplify the journey from initial grief resulting from the loss of a loved one to finding new meaning in life and improving quality of life: https://balancedwheel.co.uk

BAYO, meaning 'Joy has found us' in Yoruba, is a space to find collectives, organisations and services from across the UK – for the Black community – to support mental health and wellbeing, and it is run by the Ubele Initiative: www.BAYO.uk

Birthrights, protecting human rights in childbirth: www.birthrights.org.uk

Black Minds Matter UK (BMMUK) provides counselling support for the Black community in the UK: www.blackmindsmatteruk.com

Child Bereavement UK helps children, young people, parents and families who have been bereaved by the death of a child: www.childbereavementuk.org

Church Support Hub: Funerals, this section of the website includes the latest research thinking, resources to help at every step, ways to share ideas and the latest news and updates from funerals: www.churchsupporthub.org/funerals

Church of God of Prophecy Trust (UK): Sentient counselling: www.cogop.org.uk/sentient

Cruse Bereavement Support, helping people through one of the most painful times in life – with bereavement support, information and campaigning: www.cruse.org.uk

Haamla Service provides essential support for pregnant women and their families from minority ethnic communities, including asylum seekers and refugees, throughout their pregnancy and postnatal period: www.leedsth.nhs.uk/a-z-of-services/leeds-maternity-care/meet-the-team/haamla-service

HOPE Bereavement Support provides free and low-cost counselling, coaching and support groups for those affected by bereavement; they also provide miscarriage and child loss support groups, and a Rainbow Mamas Support group for women pregnant after a miscarriage or wanting to try again: https://hopebereavementsupport.com

Just Finance Foundation, a national charity dedicated to improving financial education for children: www.justfinancefoundation.org.uk

Living Loss, a support group for those who have lost loved ones and are bereaved: www.living-loss.org

Loss and Hope, Equipping Churches in Bereavement Support, an ecumenical project of AtaLoss working closely with key partners to help the Church support those bereaved: www.lossandhope.org

Majonzi Fund, supports members of the Black and Racialised communities who lost a loved one during Covid-19 (majonzi is Swahili for 'grief or deep sorrow'): www.majonzi-fund.com

Marie Curie, National Day of Reflection: http://dayofreflection.org.uk/

Maternity Allowance: www.gov.uk/maternity-allowance

Nafsiyat, provides therapy and counselling in 20 different languages: www.nafsiyat.org.uk

Oscar's Wish Foundation, providing support for parents, families and siblings who experience the loss of their baby: www.oscarswishfoundation.co.uk

Samaritans, a charity dedicated to reducing feelings of isolation and disconnection that can lead to suicide: www.samaritans.org

Sands, a stillbirth and neonatal death charity: www.sands.org.uk

Santé Refugee Mental Health Access Project, supporting refugees and asylum seekers in the London region, particularly those with mental health issues, to gain equal access to health and other essential services: www.santeproject.org.uk

Shout, the UK's first and only free, confidential, 24/7 text messaging support service for anyone who is struggling to cope: https://giveusashout.org

SOS Silence of Suicide, a suicide prevention and emotional wellbeing helpline: https://sossilenceofsuicide.org

Stephen Lawrence Day, an opportunity for people, communities and organisations to come together and honour Stephen's life and legacy, to stand up against discrimination, and to work towards a more hopeful tomorrow: https://stephenlawrenceday.org

The Bereavement Journey, a series of films and discussion groups that gently guide people bereaved at any time through the most common aspects of grief and bereavement: www.thebereavementjourney.org

The Lullaby Trust raises awareness of sudden infant death syndrome (SIDS), provides expert advice on safer sleep for babies and offers emotional support for bereaved families: www.lullabytrust.org.uk

The Tiny Lives Trust supports premature and sick newborn babies and their families: www.tinylives.org.uk

Tommys, researches into stillbirth, miscarriage and premature birth and provides expert support for parents before, during and after birth: www.tommys.org

Ubele Initiative, a social enterprise that supports and empowers Black and Minoritised communities in the UK to act as catalysts for social and economic change: www.ubele.org

UK Commission on Bereavement: www.bereavementcommission.org.uk

Winston's Wish, supports children in the death of a parent or sibling: www.winstonswish.org.uk

Additional resources

Books

Chimamanda Ngozi Adichie, *Notes on Grief*, London: 4th Estate, 2021. www.chimamanda.com/notes-on-grief

Joe Aldred and Keno Ogbo (eds) *The Black Church in the 21st Century*, London: Darton, Longman & Todd Ltd, 2010

Church Army, *Death, Grief & Hope: Straight Answers for Young People during the Covid-19 Pandemic* (free to download from https://churcharmy.org/be-inspired/resources)

Pete English (ed.) *Tough Stuff Journal*, a resource to help young people express and share their emotions and feelings of loss

Rio Ferdinand, *Thinking Out Loud: Love, Grief and Being Mum and Dad*, London: Hodder & Stoughton, 2017

Yasmin Gunaratnam, *Death and the Migrant: Bodies, Borders and Care*, London: Bloomsbury, 2013

Prashant Naik, *Cancer: A Journey's End*, Leicester: Matador Books, 2016

Rabbi Julia Neuberger, *Caring for Dying People of Different Faiths* (3rd edn), Boca Raton, FL: CRC Press, 2004

Colin Murray Parkes, Pittu Laungani and Bill Young (eds) *Death and Bereavement Across Cultures* (2nd edn), London: Routledge, 2015

Yvonne Richmond Tulloch, *Faith Questions in Bereavement*, The Bereavement Journey, 2020

Peter Scazzero, *The Emotionally Healthy Leader: How Transforming Your Inner Life Will Deeply Transform Your Church, Team, and the World*, Grand Rapids, MI: Zondervan, 2014

Jeffrey L. Tribble, *Transformative Pastoral Leadership in the Black Church*, New York and Basingstoke: Palgrave Macmillan, 2005

Peter M. Wherry, *Preaching Funerals in the Black Church: Bringing Perspective to Pain*, King of Prussia, PA: Judson Press, 2013

Radio
BBC Radio 5 Live, Simon Thomas interviewed by Nihal Arthanakaye: 'Kids show us something truly amazing', 20 June 2019: www.bbc.co.uk/programmes/p07dnwff

News, newspapers, magazines and factsheets

Adina Campbell, 'End-of-life care not "culturally competent"', BBC News, 15 June 2019: www.bbc.co.uk/news/health-48358492

Cruse Bereavement Care, *Bereavement Care Service Standards (BCSS)*: www. cruse.org.uk/wp-content/uploads/2021/09/Bereavement_Standards_Mar2014.pdf

Maxine Edgar, *Keep The Faith* magazine, 'Celebrating a new type of funeral', 1 June 2019: www.keepthefaith.co.uk/2019/06/01/celebrating-a-new-type-of-funeral-by-maxine-edgar (Maxine is also director of Bronze Ash Funerals: www.bronzeashfunerals.co.uk)

Organic Facts, 'Top 7 benefits of bay leaves': www.organicfacts.net/health-benefits/herbs-and-spices/bay-leaves.html

Quaker Social Action, Down to Earth, 'Funerals during the coronavirus pandemic', updated 26 July 2021: https://quakersocialaction.org.uk/we-can-help/helping-funerals/down-earth/uk-funeral-costs

Wesleyan Church UK, Pandemic Bereavement Recovery Session Two: Planning a Service of Lament with Dr Delroy Hall, 20 February 2021: www. youtube.com/watch?v=ec_CA4gP16M